Robert Burns

—◆—

SELECTED
POEMS
AND SONGS

Leaving the farm

Robert Burns

Selected Poems and Songs

Introduction by
DOUGLAS DUNN

Scottish Centre for Information and Library Services
1 John Street,
Hamilton ML3 7EU

ISBN 0 9541160 0 3

Designed by GSB Edinburgh
Printed by Nevisprint

Robt Burns

Contents

Introduction
to the
Illustrations
of
Alexander Goudie

The illustrations for this book form part of Alexander Goudie's Tam o' Shanter cycle of paintings and appear by kind permission of the artist and the South Ayrshire Council's Rozelle Gallery, Ayr where a selection of the paintings is normally on display. Further details are available on the website www.goudie.co.uk.

Goudie's complete cycle of paintings was exhibited during the Edinburgh Festival of 1996 and was hailed as a major achievement of narrative painting.

— ◆ —

List of Poems and Songs

Introduction
by
Douglas Dunn

The honorific of National Poet has been an easy one for Robert Burns's posterity to carry. Despite the irritable fervour of Christopher Murray Grieve (Hugh MacDiarmid) his monumental prestige appears invulnerable to all attempts to dismantle it in the name of turning the direction of Scottish poetry around. MacDiarmid's battle-cry of "Dunbar - not Burns!", while a salutary reminder that there is much other poetry in the Scots language (and, indeed, in English and Gaelic), as well as claims for MacDiarmid's own poetry, have left Burns invincible and untarnished. Whether a National Poet whose work expresses the life and mind of a moment of the Scottish eighteenth century can engender anything other than an inert and beautiful wonder is, however, a point worth taking seriously. Burns's poetry is direct, forthright, virtuosic in the Scots poetic forms, melodic, but short of the sensuous or mysterious imagery preferred by more recent poetic tastes, fashions, preferences, call them what you will. Just as a young Russian poet is unlikely to find Pushkin of immediate, practical assistance, or Goethe a young German, or Shakespeare a poet writing in the English language, so Burns with any young Scottish poet struggling to forge an idiom suitable for expressing the concerns of the twenty-first century. Perhaps, though, it is foolish to ask for that enabling influence from landmarks of any poetic tradition. It is enough that they exist. And if it is Burns who is your National Poet, then so much the better. He is the poet of good nature, a peculiarly pre-Modern condition, of social justice, simple religion, love, lust and appetite. As such he is as good as a homeopathic remedy to the complexities and malaises of the major props of modernism. Where the problems begin is that Burns is also the poet read for a few evenings in January by unliterary fathers prior to the annual Burns Supper with its ghastly cuisine, excessive whisky, and, worst, the address by a "celebrity". In my younger days it used to be the Chief Constable. Or an unliterary uncle, on receiving one's first collection of poems, would say, "Why do you bother? You'll never be as great as the immortal Burns." As if you didn't know. Why play football when you aren't Ian St John or Dennis Law, or Kenny Dalgleish or Jim Baxter? Why do anything? Why get up in the morning? Edwin Muir described the myth of Burns like this:

> He is more a personage to us than a poet, more a figurehead than a
> personage, and more a myth that a figurehead. To those of us who have

heard of Dunbar he is a figure, of course, comparable to Dunbar; but he is also a figurehead comparable to Prince Charlie, about whom everyone has heard. He is a myth evolved by the popular imagination, a communal poetic creation, a Protean figure; we can all shape him to our own like-ness, for a myth is endlessly adaptable.

It is poetic popularity with a vengeance. As a poet of the people, and from the people, Burns's poetry and fame, in cutting oddly across class boundaries, but appealing in particular to those with direct experience of at least some of his language, contributed to the sustenance of Scotland, or, in Renan's great phrase, to the "large scale solidarity" that is a nation. As Muir indicated clearly, the defining characteristic of Burns's fame lies in that Protean quality. So, as Muir wrote, to the respectable Burns was a decent man:

> to the Rabelaisian, bawdy; to the sentimentalist, sentimental; to the Socialist, a revolutionary; to the Nationalist, a patriot; to the religious, pious; to the self-made man, self-made; to the drinker, a drinker.

Not a lot there for a Chief Constable, you might think. You'd be wrong, of course. Among my collection of Burns editions is one printed for the Masonic Order (I'm not a member, but Burns was). Tipped in at various points through-out the book are menus and programmes of Burns Suppers covering many years, with the original owner's comments on speeches and addresses, ranging from "V. poor", to "Oh dear God, yet again, just the very same as last year", "Made a disgrace of himself", "First-class performance", "A scholar and a gen-tleman". Chief Constables, Provosts, Burgh Treasurers, Conveners of the Edu-cation Committee, and senior kirkmen appear on every occasion. Many decry the municipalized Burns or complain at the exploitation of a poet for an evening of marginal commemoration. I think they're wrong. Amazing as it may seem, there's a lot of 'amateur' but expert and sincere Burns scholarship out there among men and women for whom Burns is a serious poet and serious business. MacDiarmid's elitism found that hard to countenance. It's been my pleasure to hear first-hand accounts of Burns Suppers in pre-War British North Borneo, in POW camps in Germany (bashed neeps and tatties, nae haggis; nae whisky either), and I attended an especially dire Supper in an American city, which shall remain nameless. It was made unforgettable by ancient ladies in High-land outfits in a display of "formation walking" to music provided by a piper. He was a coal merchant of German origin whose interesting hobby was "unu-sual musical instruments". To be candid, I find it exhilarating that a Scottish poet should be remembered almost everywhere, and the Scots language spo-ken on these occasions. Personally, I find Burns Suppers a pain in the neck, if only because I've been obliged to speak at them. The favoured celebration is with a few like-minded friends and a bottle (or two) of Springbank on 25th January, which is a bit damaging as it is soon after New Year while Byron's equally deserving birthday falls on the 22nd.

For the "respectable" or decent, Burns's "The Cotter's Saturday Night" is

Burns's birthplace

possibly the poem to which they return most frequently, although I doubt if they leave it at that. In my experience, the overtly respectable often possess covert tastes in the very opposite to what you expect. Burns's celebration of hearth and family now strikes most readers as pious and sentimental, while scholars tend to see in it the origins of what came to be known in the late nineteenth century as the Kailyard. It can be seen, though, as Burns's idealistic anchor in the virtue of his people:

> The cheerfu' Supper done, wi' serious face,
> They, round the ingle, form a circle wide;
> The Sire turns o'er, with patriarchal grace,
> The big *ha' Bible* ance his *Father's* pride:
> His bonnet rev'rently is laid aside,
> His *lyart haffets* wearing thin and bare;
> Those strains that once did sweet in ZION glide,
> He wales a portion with judicious care;
> *'And let us worship GOD!'* he says with solemn air.

Signposted Scots diction in the Spenserian stanza, which had enjoyed a vogue in mid-eighteenth century Britain, helps to highlight the piety of what exercises Burns in "The Cotter's Saturday Night". He was up to a poetic stunt, just to prove he could do it; he was also proving his roots in rural and national virtue, as if to show what he would depart from, and also what he would never compromise. Although a poem loaded with many problems of sentiment, it is also important within Burns's canon. Encoded within it and often on its surface is a portrayal of social order dependent on the family, an awareness of hierarchy as well as a contrasting dismissal of social distinctions and inherited titles, and an approval of Union with England. Such sentiments are especially clear in the last three stanzas, by which time Burns has modulated into an elevated and rhetorical English idiom.

A Rabelaisian or bawdy Burns coexists but contends with the poet of "The Cotter's Saturday Night". It threads through Burns's poetry, but "The Holy Fair" can stand as a clear example. The occasion evoked is the annual parish communion day in Mauchline in Ayrshire. Sanctioned by tradition, it was taken as an opportunity for fun, games and serious drinking as well as religious observation. Anonymous fifteenth/sixteenth century carnivalesque poems, "Christ's Kirk on the Green" and "Peblis to the Play", provide the origin of the lively stanza, probably written to be sung, and which had been adapted earlier by Robert Fergusson. Ribaldry is distributed throughout the poem as part of Burns's satirical exposure of hypocrisy (perfected in "Holy Willie's Prayer") but also in his apparent role as a Lord of Misrule (see, especially, "Love and Liberty", or the verses and songs collected posthumously as *The Merry Muses of Caledonia*). Fun *versus* Hypocrisy, like Social Justice *versus* Tyranny, is part of a syndrome of antitheses and antagonisms essential to Burns. Some bawdy moments are half-buried in fancy language, as in "cantharidian plaisters" (stanza xiii) which are said to "fire the heart devout". Cantharid is spanish-fly, the famous or notorious aphrodisiac. Religious rhapsody, then, is associated with contrived sexual excitement; or, as he says more tantalizingly towards the end of the poem:

> Wi *faith*, an' *hope*, an *love* an' *drink*
> They're a' in famous tune
> For crack that day.

Piety, desire, and high-spirited inebriation - it appears an unorthodox trinity but reflected the customs of rural, Lowland life. By the last stanza he is more explicit:

> How monie hearts this day converts,
> O' Sinners and o' Lasses!
> Their hearts o' stane, gin night are gane
> As saft as ony flesh is.
> There's some are fou' o' *love divine*;
> There's some are fou' o' *brandy*;
> An' monie jobs that day begin,
> May end in *Houghmagandie*
> Some ither day.

Burns is winking slyly at the reader and smiling broadly - he is showing how communities perpetuate themselves through their festive rituals, and he is as tolerant of the pious as he is encouraging of the amorous. After such a hectic performance it can be imagined that the speaker/singer is sweating as well. "Some ither day" could be ironic, meaning not what it says, but "very soon" or "right this minute". Burns was no Lawrentian sexual theorist or cajoler; he was a participant.

Mock Elegy, which contemplates the deaths or misfortunes of persons or creatures lower in the social or natural order than the poet, introduces the element of Burns's poetry often described as "sentimental". "The sentimental structure of benevolent condescension", as Professor McGuirk calls it (in her *Robert Burns and the Sentimental Era*, 1985), is evident in "To a Mouse, On Turning her up in her Nest, with the Plough, November 1785".

> Wee, sleeket, cowran, tim'rous *beastie*,
> O, what a panic's in thy breastie!
> Thou need na start awa sae hasty,
>> Wi' bickering brattle!
> I wad be laith to rin an' chase thee,
>> Wi murd'ring *pattle*!

Small, vulnerable, pathetic, the mouse is also the object of Burns's benevolent familiarity and amusement. By the second stanza Burns is apologizing for man's sovereignty over Nature, and associating his own mortality with that of a diminutive fellow creature. Although the mouse may be a crop-nibbler, it's on such a small scale that co-existence is easy to exercise. What's an ear or two of corn among fellow creatures? The fourth, fifth and sixth stanzas extend the conventional pathos of the poem through pity for the mouse's predicament - homeless, and winter coming on. By the last two stanzas, it becomes clear that although the poet's attention is fixed on a mouse, his purpose is to lament the unexpectedness of life and its possible misfortunes. They contain one of Burns's most quoted passages:

> But *Mousie*, thou art no thy-lane,
> In proving *foresight* may be vain:
> The best-laid schemes o' *Mice* an' *Men*
>> Gang aft agley,
> An' lea'e us nought but grief an' pain,
>> For promis'd joy!
>
> Still, thou art blest, compar'd wi' *me*!
> The *present* only toucheth thee:
> But Och! I *backward* cast my e'e,
>> On prospects drear!
> An' *forward*, tho' I canna *see*,
>> I *guess* and *fear*!

Famously, Burns is the poet of the Common Man. His libertarian political passion can be seen to underwrite almost all his work. It is proclaimed as an aesthetic principle in "The Vision", and in "Epistle to J. Lapraik, An Old Scotch Bard" where this memorable passage of five stanzas can be taken to illustrate his loyalty to locality and fearlessness before the "authority" of High Culture:

> I am nae Poet, in a sense,
> But just a *Rhymer* like by chance,
> An' hae to Learning nae pretence,
>> Yet, what the matter?

Whene'er my Muse does on me glance,
　　　I jingle at her.

Your Critic-folk may cock their nose,
And say, 'How can you e'er propose,
'You wha ken hardly *verse* frae *prose*,
　　　'To mak a *sang*?'
But by your leaves, my learned foes,
　　　Ye're maybe wrang.

What 's a' jargon o' your Schools,
Your Latin names for horns an' stools;
If honest Nature made you *fools*,
　　　What sairs your Grammars?
Ye'd better ten up spades and *shools*,
　　　Or *knappin-hammers*.

A set o' dull, conceited Hashes,
Confuse their brains in *Colledge-classes!*
They *gang* in Stirks, and *come out* Asses,
　　　Plain truth to speak;
An' syne they think to climb Parnassus
　　　By dint o' Greek!

Gie me ae spark o' Nature's fire,
That's a' the learning I desire;
Then tho' I drudge thro' dub an' mire
　　　At pleugh or cart,
My Muse, tho' hamely in attire,
　　　May touch the heart.

Personally, I find no difficulty in connecting these ground-clearing poetic statements of 1785 with the post-French Revolution fervour of the song "For a' that and a' that" ("Is there, for honest Poverty") of January 1795. A poet's politics are usually inseparable from his or her poetry, where, that is, a poet is other than apolitical.

Is there, for honest Poverty
　　　That hings his head, and a' that;
The coward-slave, we pass him by,
　　　We dare be poor for a' that!
For a' that, and a' that,
　　　Our toils obscure, and a' that,
The rank is but the guinea's stamp,
　　　The Man's the gowd for a' that. -

Burns's politics caused him discomfort. As an officer of the Excise he was beholden to orthodox elements in Scottish and British society and obliged to apologize more than once for political expressions that did not endear him to them. Within weeks of writing "For a' that" he also wrote "The Dumfries Volunteers":

> Does haughty Gaul invasion threat?
> > Then let the loons beware, Sir!
> There's wooden walls upon our seas
> > And volunteers on shore, Sir!

Enthusiasm, compromise, or self-preservation? A mixture of all three, perhaps, but redeemed - if that's the term - by the closing lines:

> Who will not sing *God save the King*
> > Shall hang as high's the steeple;
> But while we sing *God save the King*,
> > We'll ne'er forget the People!

Burns thrilled to the names and deeds of Wallace and Robert the Bruce, the heroes of the Scottish Wars of Independence. "Scots, Wha Hae", once Scotland's anthem, dates from 1793 and is best seen as a national expression of his post-Revolution politics. His patriotism is perhaps best described by his song collecting, for which he refused all payment, his use of Scots language, and his reliance in his best work on traditional Scottish measures and forms.

Burns associated himself with the liberal or New Licht tendency in the Church of Scotland. "Address to the Unco Guid, or the Rigidly Righteous" (the long title, and alliteration, spoof the style of extremist presbyterian pamphleteers) satirizes Auld Licht adherents, champions of such Calvinist notions as predestination. That the epigraph is versified scripture shows Burns attempting to enlist Biblical authority in support of his argument. Mounted with forensic organization, the poem reads like a speech by an advocate for the pursuer, and the Unco Guid arraigned in court as defenders or pursued. As in "Holy Willie's Prayer" or "The Holy Fair" Burns's momentum is explained by his loathing of cant and hypocrisy, and his fundamental belief that "An honest man's the noblest work of God".

Burns was so intimate with the "song culture" of eighteenth-century Scotland that it resulted in almost all of his poems being instinctively or deliberately calculated for performance. Vocal modulations, the sonic resonances of Scots diction, traditional Scots verse forms masterfully revived, contribute to the hilarious brilliance of "Holy Willie's Prayer" just as they account for the success of so many others of his poems:

> O thou that in the heavens does dwell!
> Wha, as it pleases best thysel,
> Sends ane to heaven and ten to h-ll,
> > A' for thy glory!
> And no for ony gude or ill
> > They've done before thee. -

Holy Willie as a self-chosen member of the Elect proceeds to expose himself as a deluded humbug or wilful fake.

One of the greatest self-made men ever, Andrew Carnegie, was an admirer of Burns. But the poet did not earn a fortune from his work. Instead, it led to a demanding if also sociable day-job in the Excise at a stipend that was above that of a contemporary schoolmaster or minister of the Kirk. He also maintained the farm of Ellisland on the side as a hedge against the insecurity of continuing to be acceptable to the powers-that-be. But this is really a bigger issue than Edwin Muir makes out. It rubs against the brittleness of Burns's political position after 1789, while any reader who thinks of Burns's career must constantly be reminded of how he was never in a position to live off his *poetry*. There is also the chosen unrewardedness of his industry in song-collecting and editing to consider. Self-made in this context means that he made himself into a poet out of local materials in the way described in "Epistle to J. Lapraik" and "A Vision". It amounted to an advancement which Burns and his family may well have felt to be decisive if also onerous; but it was far from a carefree prosperity with ample leisure and time for writing.

Was Burns distracted by drink? Such is the solidity of his technique and productivity in a relatively short life that no one could claim that it shows. Much of his verse, such as "Scotch Drink", is rinsed in praise of heavy water, though:

> O *Whisky*! soul o' plays and pranks!
> Accept a *Bardie's* gratefu' thanks!
> When wanting thee, what tuneless cranks
>   Are my poor Verses!
> Thou comes - they rattle i' their ranks
>   At ither's arses!

After a hard day of farm work, or fulfilling his duties in the Dumfries district's Excise, and covering considerable territory it is, of course, possible that Burns "needed" alcohol to enliven his pen. Two stanzas later, he denounces Excisemen:

> Thae curst horse-leeches o' th' Excise,
> Wha mak' the Whisky *stills* their prize!

He became one not long after. It didn't change him. "Tam o' Shanter" could be read as a tongue-in-cheek morality tale of the evils of drink. No doubt it has been, and still is, but the obviousness of the admonitory ending is of a piece with the pleasurable artifice of the narrative. Edwin Muir's pigeon-holing descriptions of aspects of Burns and his poetry which appeal to different kinds of people is not exhaustive. One obvious omission is Burns as a storyteller, and everyone likes a story. Many of his poems have striking occasions, in themselves nuggets of narrative - "To a Louse", "To a Mouse", "The Twa Dogs", "The Holy Fair", "Halloween". It is an enabling dimension of his work, one which makes it accessible.

Burns the amorist is another category (but we should beware of "categories") which eluded Muir. He is one of the great love-lyricists of poetry. In his oft-quoted letter of August 1787 to Dr John Moore he wrote candidly of "a certain delicious Passion ... I hold to be the first of human joys, our dearest pleasure here below". "Thus began with me Love and Poetry," he wrote later in the same letter. Love, sex and poetry were inseparable pleasures for Burns. Many of his songs are for a female voice ("John Anderson my Jo", "My Tochers the Jewel", "Ay Waukin O", "I'm o'er Young to Marry Yet", "The Rantin Dog the Daddie o' t"), others for a male voice, some, on the moods of love, easily transferable from one to another. Notoriously, or famously, Burns was an amorous man, and his fascination for Scots song was more than antiquarian. The name of Burns brings tunes to the mind as well as verses - "My Luve is Like a Red Red Rose", "Ae Fond Kiss", "Green Grow the Rashes", "O Whistle and I'll Come to Ye, My Lad", "For a' that an' a' that", "Auld Lang Syne". Of how many poets can that be said?

If you take all these features of Burns, add others, mix them while leaving room for the unpredictable, then you begin to see at least something of his achievement. Include, especially, his skill in traditional Scots verse forms - Standard Habbie, variations on the Christ's Kirk stanza and the verse of Montgomerie's "The Cherrie and the Slae", Ballade Royal, iambic tetrameter couplets, the cadenced fashioning of song lyrics - then what ought to be recognized is Burns's astonishing *artistry* which his ironically bashful accounts of his status in "Epistle to J. Lapraik" and "A Vision" disguise as rustic craftsmanship. It is that level of artistry, passionate expression, variety of interest, candour, and good nature, which an aspiring poet in Scotland (or, indeed, anywhere) might want to emulate. Modernity, however, will prove a powerful inhibition.

Douglas Dunn
Professor, School of English,
St Andrews University

Ilk man and mother's son take heed

SELECTED POEMS AND SONGS

Duncan Gray

Duncan Gray cam here to woo,
Ha, ha, the wooing o't,
On blythe Yule night when we were fu',
Ha, ha, the wooing o't,
Maggie coost her head fu' high,
Look'd asklent and unco skiegh,
Gart poor Duncan stand abiegh;
Ha, ha, the wooing o't.

Duncan fleech'd, and Duncan pray'd;
Ha, ha, the wooing o't,
Meg was deaf as Ailsa Craig,
Ha, ha, the wooing o't,
Duncan sigh'd baith out and in,
Grat his een baith bleer't and blin',
Spak o' lowpin o'er a linn;
Ha, ha, the wooing o't.

Time and Chance are but a tide,
Ha, ha, the wooing o't,
Slighted love is sair to bide,
Ha, ha, the wooing o't,
Shall I, like a fool, quoth he,
For a haughty hizzie die?
She may gae to – France for me!
Ha, ha, the wooing o't.

How it comes let Doctors tell,
Ha, ha, the wooing o't,
Meg grew sick – as he grew heal,
Ha, ha, the wooing o't,
Something in her bosom wrings,
For relief a sigh she brings;
And O her een, they spak sic things!
Ha, ha, the wooing o't.

Duncan was a lad o'grace,
Ha, ha, the wooing o't,
Maggie's was a piteous case,
Ha, ha, the wooing o't,
Duncan could na be her death,
Swelling Pity smoor'd his Wrath;
Now they're crouse and canty baith.
Ha, ha, the wooing o't.

The Banks O' Doon

Ye banks and braes o' bonie Doon,
How can ye bloom sae fresh and fair;
How can ye chant, ye little birds,
And I sae weary, fu' o' care!
Thou'll break my heart, thou warbling bird,
That wanton's thro' the flowering thorn:
Thou minds me o' departed joys,
Departed never to return. —

Oft hae I rov'd by bonie Doon,
To see the rose and woodbine twine;
And ilka bird sang o' its Luve,
And fondly sae did I o' mine. —
Wi' lightsome heart I pu'd a rose,
Fu' sweet upon its thorny tree;
And my fause Luver staw my rose,
But, ah! he left the thorn wi' me. —

O, wert thou in the cauld blast

O, wert thou in the cauld blast,
On yonder lea, on yonder lea;
My plaidie to the angry airt,
I'd shelter thee, I'd shelter thee:
Or did misfortune's bitter storms
Around thee blaw, around thee blaw,
Thy bield should be my bosom,
To share it a', to share it a'.

Or were I in the wildest waste,
Sae black and bare, sae black and bare,
The desert were a paradise,
 If thou wert there, if thou wert there.
Or were I monarch o' the globe,
Wi' thee to reign, wi' thee to reign;
The brightest jewel in my crown,
Wad be my queen, wad be my queen.

John Anderson, my jo

John Anderson my jo, John,
When we were first acquent;
Your locks were like the raven,
Your bony brow was brent;
But now your brow is beld, John,
Your locks are like the snaw;
But blessings on your frosty pow,
John Anderson my jo.

John Anderson my jo, John,
We clamb the hill thegither;
And mony a canty day, John,
We've had wi' ane anither;
Now we maun totter down, John,
And hand in hand we'll go;
And sleep thegither at the foot,
John Anderson my jo.

A Poet's Welcome to His Love-Begotten Daughter

THE FIRST INSTANCE THAT ENTITLED HIM TO THE VENERABLE
APPELLATION OF FATHER

Thou's welcome, Wean! Mischanter fa' me,
If thoughts o' thee, or yet thy mamie,
Shall ever daunton me or awe me.
      My bonie lady,
Or if I blush when thou shalt ca' me
      Tyta or Daddie.

Tho' now they ca' me Fornicator,
An' tease my name in countra clatter,
The mair they talk, I'm kend the better,
      E'en let them clash;
An auld wife's tongue's a feckless matter
      To gie ane fash.

Welcome! my bonie, sweet, wee Dochter,
Tho' ye come here a wee unsought for,
And tho' your comin' I hae fought for,
      Baith Kirk and Queir;
Yet, by my faith, ye're no unwrought for,
      That I shall swear!

Sweet fruit o' monie a merry dint,
My funny toil is no a' tint,
Tho' thou cam to the warld asklent,
      Which fools may scoff at;
In my last plack thy part's be in't
      The better half o't.

Tho' I should be the waur bestead,
Thou's be as braw and bienly clad,
And thy young years as nicely bred
      Wi' education,
As onie brat o' Wedlock's bed,
      In a' thy station.

Wee image o' my bonie Betty,
As fatherly I kiss and daut thee,
As dear and near my heart I set thee
      Wi' as gude will
As a' the priests had seen me get thee
      That's out o' Hell.

Lord grant that thou may aye inherit
Thy mither's person, grace, an' merit,
An' thy poor, worthless daddy's spirit,
      Without his failins,
'Twill please me mair to see thee heir it,
      Than stockit mailens.

For if thou be what I wad hae thee,
An' tak the counsel I shall gie thee,
I'll never rue my trouble wi' thee-
      The cost nor shame o't,
But be a loving father to thee,
      And brag the name o't.

Epitaph on a Wag in Mauchline

Lament 'im Mauchline husbands a',
He aften did assist ye;
For had ye staid whole weeks awa'
Your wives they ne'er had miss'd ye.

Ye Mauchline bairns as on ye pass,
To school in bands thegither,
O tread ye lightly on his grass,
Perhaps he was your father.

As market days are wearing late

The Lovely Lass of Inverness

The lovely lass o' Inverness,
Nae joy nor pleasure can she see;
For e'en and morn she cries, Alas!
And ay the saut tear blins her e'e.
Drumossie moor, Drumossie day,
A waefu' day it was to me;
For there I lost my father dear,
My father dear and brethren three.

Their winding-sheet the bludy clay,
Their graves are growing green to see;
And by them lies the dearest lad
That ever blest a woman's e'e!
Now wae to thee, thou cruel lord,
A bludy man I trow thou be;
For mony a heart thou has made sair
That ne'er did wrang to thine or thee!

The Holy Fair

A robe of seeming truth and trust
Hid crafty Observation;
And secret hung, with poison'd crust,
The dirk of Defamation:
A mask that like the gorget show'd,
Dye-varying on the pigeon;
And for a mantle large and broad,
He wrapt him in Religion.
     (Hypocrisy a-la-Mode)

    I

Upon a simmer *Sunday morn*,
When Nature's face is fair,
I walked forth to view the corn,
An' snuff the caller air.
The rising sun, owre Galston muirs,
Wi' glorious light was glintin;
The hares were hirplin down the furrs,
The lav'rocks they were chantin
     Fu' sweet that day.

II

As lightsomely I glower'd abroad,
    To see a scene sae gay,
Three *hizzies*, early at the road,
    Cam skelpin up the way.
Twa had manteeles o' dolefu' black,
    But ane wi' lyart lining:
The *third*, that gaed a wee a-back,
    Was in the fashion shining
        Fu' gay that day.

III

The *twa* appear'd like sisters twin,
    In feature, form, an' claes;
Their visage – wither'd, lang an' thin,
    An' sour as ony slaes:
The *third* cam up, hap-step-an'-lowp,
    As light as ony lambie,
An' wi' a curchie low did stoop,
    As soon as e'er she saw me,
        Fu' kind that day.

IV

Wi' bonnet aff, quoth I, 'Sweet lass,
    I think ye seem to ken me;
I'm sure I've seen that bonie face,
    But yet I canna name ye.'
Quo' she, an' laughin as she spak,
    An' taks me by the hauns,
'Ye, for my sake, hae gi'en the feck
    Of a' the *ten commands*
        A screed some day.'

V

'My name is Fun—your cronie dear,
    The nearest friend ye hae;
An' this is Superstition here,
    An' that's Hypocrisy.
I'm gaun to *Mauchline Holy Fair*,
    To spend an hour in daffin:
Gin ye'll go there, yon runkl'd pair,
    We will get famous laughin
        At them this day.'

VI

Quoth I, 'With a' my heart, I'll do't;
I'll get my Sunday's sark on,
An' meet you on the holy spot;
Faith, we'se hae fine remarkin!'
Then I gaed hame at crowdie-time,
An' soon I made me ready;
For roads were clad, frae side to side,
Wi' monie a wearie body,
        In droves that day.

VII

Here, farmers gash, in ridin graith,
Gaed hoddin by their cotters;
There, swankies young, in braw braid-claith,
Are springin owre the gutters.
The lasses, skelpin barefit, thrang,
In silks an' scarlets glitter;
Wi' *sweet-milk cheese*, in monie a whang,
An' *farls*, bak'd wi' butter,
        Fu' crump that day.

VIII

When by the *plate* we set our nose,
Weel heaped up wi' ha'pence,
A greedy glowr *Black Bonnet* throws,
An' we maun draw our tippence.
Then in we go to see the show,
On ev'ry side they're gath'rin;
Some carryin dails, some chairs an' stools,
An' some are busy bleth'rin
        Right loud that day.

IX

Here stands a shed to fend the show'rs,
An' screen our countra Gentry,
There, *Races-Jess*, an' twa-three whores,
Are blinkin at the entry.
Here sits a raw o' tittlin jads,
Wi' heaving breast an' bare neck;
An' there, a batch o' *wabster lads*,
Blackguarding frae Kilmarnock
        For *fun* this day.

X

Here some are thinkin on their sins,
An' some upo' their claes;
Ane curses feet that fyl'd his shins,
Anither sighs an' prays:
On this hand sits a Chosen swatch,
Wi' screw'd-up, grace-proud faces;
On that, a set o' chaps, at watch,
Thrang winkin on the lasses
        To *chairs* that day.

XI

O happy is that man an' blest!
Nae wonder that it pride him!
Wha's ain dear lass, that he likes best,
Comes clinkin down beside him!
Wi' arm repos'd on the *chair-back*,
He sweetly does compose him;
Which, by degrees, slips round her *neck*,
An's loof upon her *bosom*
        Unkend that day.

XII

Now a' the congregation o'er
Is silent expectation;
For Moodie speels the holy door,
Wi' tidings o' damnation.
Should *Hornie*, as in ancient days,
'Mang sons o' God present him,
The vera sight o' Moodie's face.
To's ain *het hame* had sent him
        Wi' fright that day.

XIII

Hear how he clears the points o' Faith
Wi' rattlin an' thumpin!
Now meekly calm, now wild in wrath.
He's stampin, an' he's jumpin!
His lengthen'd chin, his turn'd-up snout,
His eldritch squeel an' gestures,
O how they fire the heart devout,
Like cantharidian plasters,
        On sic a day!

XIV

But hark! the *tent* has chang'd its voice;
There's peace an' rest nae langer:
For a' the *real judges* rise,
They canna sit for anger.
Smith opens out his cauld harangues,
On *practice* and on *morals*;
An' aff the godly pour in thrangs,
To gie the jars an' barrels
          A lift that day.

XV

What signifies his barren shine,
Of *moral* pow'rs an' *reason*?
His English style, an' gesture fine,
Are a' clean out o' season.
Like Socrates or Antonine,
Or some auld pagan Heathen,
The *moral man* he does define,
But ne'er a word o' *faith* in
          That's right that day.

XVI

In guid time comes an antidote
Against sic poison'd nostrum;
For Peebles, frae the water-fit,
Ascends the *holy rostrum*:
See, up he's got the word o' God,
An' meek an' mim has view'd it,
While Common-Sense has taen the road,
An' aff, an' up the *Cowgate*
          Fast, fast that day.

XVII

Wee Miller niest, the Guard relieves,
An' Orthodoxy raibles,
Tho' in his heart he weel believes,
An' thinks it auld wives' fables:
But faith! the birkie wants a *Manse*,
So, cannilie he hums them;
Altho' his *carnal* wit an' sense
Like hafflins-wise o'ercomes him
          At times that day.

XVIII

Now, butt an' ben the Change-house fills,
Wi' *yill-caup* Commentators:
Here's crying out for bakes an' gills,
An' there the pint-stowp clatters;
While thick an' thrang, an' loud an' lang,
Wi' Logic, an' wi' *Scripture*,
They raise a din, that, in the end,
Is like to breed a rupture
        O' wrath that day.

XIX

Leeze me on Drink! it gies us mair
Than either School or Colledge:
It kindles Wit, it waukens Leas,
It pangs us fou o' Knowledge.
Be't *whisky gill* or *penny wheep*,
Or ony stronger potion,
It never fails, on drinkin deep,
To kittle up our *notion*,
        By night or day.

XX

The lads an' lasses, blythely bent
To mind baith *saul* an' *body*,
Sit round the table, weel content,
An' steer about the *Toddy*.
On this ane's dress, an' that ane's leuk,
They're makin observations;
While some are cozie i' the neuk,
An' formin *assignations*
        To meet some day.

XXI

But now the Lord's ain trumpet touts,
Till a' the hills are rairin,
An' echos back return the shouts;
Black Russell is na spairin:
His piercing words, like Highlan swords,
Divide the joints an' marrow;
His talk o' Hell, whare devils dwell,
Our vera 'sauls does harrow'
        Wi' fright that day!

XXII

A vast, unbottom'd, boundless *Pit*,
Fill'd fou o' *lowin brunstane*,
Wha's ragin flame, an' scorchin heat,
Wad melt the hardest whun-stane!
The *half-asleep* start up wi' fear,
An' think they hear it roarin,
When presently it does appear,
'Twas but some neebor *snorin*
        Asleep that day.

XXIII

'Twad be owre lang a tale to tell,
How monie stories past,
An' how they crouded to the yill,
When they were a' dismist:
How drink gaed round, in cogs an' caups,
Amang the furms an' benches;
An' *cheese* an' *bread*, frae women's laps,
Was dealt about in lunches,
        An' dawds that day.

XXIV

In comes a gausie, gash *Guidwife*,
An' sits down by the fire,
Syne draws her *kebbuck* an' her knife,
The lasses they are shyer.
The auld *Guidmen*, about the *grace*,
Frae side to side they bother,
Till some ane by his bonnet lays,
An' gies them't, like a *tether*,
        Fu' lang that day.

XXV

Wae sucks! for him that gets nae lass,
Or lasses that hae naething!
Sma' need has he to say a grace.
Or melvie his braw claithing!
O *Wives* be mindfu', ance yoursel
How bonie lads ye wanted,
An' dinna, for a *kebbuck-heel*,
Let lasses be affronted
        On sic a day!

XXVI

Now *Clinkumbell*, wi' rattlin tow,
Begins to jow an' croon;
Some swagger hame, the best they dow,
Some wait the afternoon.
At slaps the billies halt a blink,
Till lasses strip their shoon:
Wi *faith* an' *hope*, an' *love* an' *drink*.
They're a' in famous tune
      For crack that day.

XXVII

How monie hearts this day converts
O' Sinners and o' Lasses!
Their hearts o' stane, gin night are gane,
As saft as ony flesh is.
There's some are fou o' *love divine*;
There's some are fou o' *brandy*;
An' monie jobs that day begin,
May end in *Houghmagandie*
      Some ither day.

To a Mouse

ON TURNING HER UP IN HER NEST, WITH THE PLOUGH,
NOVEMBER 1785

Wee, sleekit, cowran, tim'rous *beastie*,
O, what a panic's in thy breastie!
Thou need na start awa sae hasty,
    Wi' bickering brattle!
I wad be laith to rin an' chase thee,
    Wi' murd'ring *pattle*!

I'm truly sorry Man's dominion
Has broken Nature's social union,
An' justifies that ill opinion,
    Which makes thee startle,
At me, thy poor, earth-born companion,
    An' *fellow-mortal*!

I doubt na, whyles, but thou may *thieve*;
What then? poor beastie, thou maun live!
A *daimen-icker* in a *thrave*
    'S a sma' request.
I'll get a blessin wi' the lave,
    An' never miss't!

Thy wee-bit *housie*, too, in ruin!
Its silly wa's the win's are strewin!
An naething, now, to big a new ane,
    O' foggage green!
An' bleak *December's winds* ensuin,
    Baith snell an' keen!

Thou saw the fields laid bare an' wast,
An' weary *Winter* comin fast,
An' cozie here, beneath the blast,
    Thou thought to dwell,
Till crash! the cruel *coulter* past
    out thro' thy cell.

That wee-bit heap o' leaves an stibble
Has cost thee monie a weary nibble!
Now thou's turn'd out, for a' thy trouble,
    But house or hald,
To thole the Winter's *sleety dribble*,
    An' *cranreuch* cauld!

But, Mousie, thou art no thy-lane,
In proving *foresight* may be vain:
The best-laid schemes o' *Mice* an' *Men*
    Gang aft agley,
An' lea'e us nought but grief an' pain,
    For promis'd joy!

Still, thou art blest, compar'd wi' *me*!
The *present* only toucheth thee:
But, Och! I *backward* cast my e'e
    On prospects drear!
An' *forward*, tho' I canna *see*,
    I *guess* an' *fear*!

Epistle to J. Lapraik

AN OLD SCOTTISH BARD

While briers an' woodbines budding green,
And paitricks scraichin loud at e'en,
An' morning poosie whiddin seen,
  Inspire my Muse,
This freedom, in an *unknown* frien',
  I pray excuse.

On Fasten-een we had a rockin,
To ca' the crack and weave our stockin;
And there was muckle fun and jokin,
  Ye need na doubt;
At length we had a hearty yokin
  At *sang about*.

There was ae *sang*, amang the rest,
Aboon them a' it pleas'd me best,
That some kind husband had addrest
  To some sweet wife:
It thirl'd the heart-strings thro' the breast,
  A' to the life.

I've scarce heard ought describ'd sae weel,
What gen'rous, manly bosoms feel;
Thought I, 'Can this be Pope or Steele,
Or *Beattie's* wark?'
They told me 'twas an odd kind chiel
  About Muirkirk.

It pat me fidgin-fain to hear't,
An' sae about him there I spier't;
Then a' that ken't him round declar'd,
  He had *ingine*,
That nane excell'd it, few cam near't,
  It was sae fine.

That set him to a pint of ale,
An' either douce or merry tale,
Or rhymes an' sangs he'd made himsel.
  Or witty catches,
'Tween Inverness and Tiviotdale,
  He had few matches.

Then up I gat, an' swoor an aith,
Tho' I should pawn my pleugh an' graith,
Or die a cadger pownie's death,
    At some dyke-back
A *pint* an' *gill* I'd gie them *baith*,
    To hear your crack.

But, first an' foremost, I should tell,
Amaist as soon as I could spell,
I to the *crambo-jingle* fell,
    Tho' rude an' rough,
Yet crooning to a body's sel,
    Does weel eneugh.

I am nae *Poet*, in a sense,
But just a *Rhymer*, like, by chance,
An' hae to Learning nae pretence,
    Yet, what the matter?
Whene'er my Muse does on me glance,
    I jingle at her.

Your Critic-folk may cock their nose,
And say, 'How can you e'er propose,
You wha ken hardly verse frae prose,
    To mak a sang?'
But, by your leaves, my learned foes,
    Ye're maybe wrang.

What's a' your jargon o' your Schools,
Your Latin names for horns an' stools;
If honest Nature made you *fools*,
    What sairs your Grammars?
Ye'd better taen up *spades* and *shools*,
    Or *knappin-hammers*.

A set o' dull, conceited Hashes,
Confuse their brains in *Colledge-classes*!
They *gang* in Stirks, and *come* out Asses,
    Plain truth to speak;
An' syne they think to climb Parnassus
    By dint o' Greek!

Gie me ae spark o' Nature's fire,
That's a' the learning I desire;
Then tho' I drudge thro' dub an' mire
    At pleugh or cart,

My Muse, tho' hamely in attire,
      May touch the heart.

O for a spunk o' Allan's glee,
Or Fergusson's, the bauld an' slee,
Or bright Lapraik's, my friend to be,
      If I can hit it!
That would be *lear* eneugh for me,
      If I could get it.

Now, Sir, if ye hae friends enow,
Tho' *real friends* I b'lieve are few,
Yet, if your catalogue be fou,
      I'se no insist;
But gif ye want ae friend that's true,
      I'm on your list.

I winna blaw about *mysel*,
As ill I like my fauts to tell;
But friends an' folks that wish me well,
      They sometimes roose me;
Tho' I maun own, as monie still
      As far abuse me.

There's ae *wee faut* they whyles lay to me,
I like the lasses – Gude forgie me!
For monie a plack they wheedle frae me,
      At dance or fair;
Maybe some *ither thing* they gie me
      They weel can spare.

But Mauchline Race or Mauchline Fair,
I should be proud to meet you there;
We'se gie ae night's discharge to *care*,
      If we forgather,
An' hae a swap o' *rhymin-ware*
      Wi' ane anither.

The *four-gill* chap, we'se gar him clatter,
An' kirsen him wi' reekin water;
Syne we'll sit down an' tak our whitter,
      To chear our heart;
An' faith, we'se be *acquainted* better
      Before we part.

Awa ye selfish, warly race,
Wha think that havins, sense, an' grace,
Ev'n love an' friendship, should give place
      To *catch-the-plack*!
I dinna like to see your face,
      Nor hear your crack.

But ye whom social pleasure charms,
Whose hearts the *tide of kindness* warms,
Who hold your *being* on the terms,
      'Each aid the others,'
Come to my bowl, come to my arms,
      My friends, my brothers!

But to conclude my lang epistle,
As my auld pen's worn to the grissle;
Twa lines frae you wad gar me fissle,
      Who am, most fervent,
While I can either sing, or whissle,
      Your friend and servant.

My love, she's but a lassie yet

My love she's but a lassie yet,
My love she's but a lassie yet,
We'll let her stand a year or twa,
She'll no be half sae saucy yet.

I rue the day I sought her O,
I rue the day I sought her O,
Wha gets her needs na say he's woo'd,
But he may say he's bought her O.

Come draw a drap o' the best o't yet,
Come draw a drap o' the best o't yet:
Gae seek for pleasure whare ye will.
But here I never misst it yet.

We're a' dry wi' drinking o't,
We're a' dry wi' drinking o't:
The minister kisst the fidler's wife,
He could na preach for thinkin o't.

There was a lad

There was a lad was born in Kyle,
But whatna day o' whatna style,
I doubt it's hardly worth the while,
To be sae nice wi' Robin.

Chorus

Robin was a rovin' boy
Rantin' rovin', rantin' rovin',
Robin was a rovin' boy
Rantin' rovin' Robin!

Our monarch's hindmost year but ane
Was five-and-twenty days begun,
'Twas then a blast o' Janwar' Win'
Blew hansel in on Robin.
Robin was, &c.

The gossip keekit in his loof,
Quo' scho, 'Wha lives will see the proof,
This waly boy will be nae coof,
I think we'll ca' him Robin.
Robin was, &c.

'He'll hae misfortunes great and sma',
But ay a heart aboon them a';
He'll be a credit 'till us a',
We'll a' be proud o' Robin.
Robin was, &c.

'But sure as three times three mak' nine,
I see by ilka score and line,
This chap will dearly like our kin',
So leeze me on thee, Robin'.
Robin was, &c.

'Gude faith,' quo' scho, 'I doubt you gar
The bonie lasses lie aspar;
But twenty fauts ye may hae waur,
So blessins on thee, Robin!'
Robin was, &c.

To a Louse

ON SEEING ONE ON A LADY'S BONNET AT CHURCH

Ha! whare ye gaun, ye crowlin ferlie!
Your impudence protects you sairlie:
I canna say but ye strunt rarely,
   Owre *gauze* and *lace*;
Tho' faith, I fear, ye dine but sparely
   On sic a place.

Ye ugly, creepin, blastit wonner,
Detested, shunn'd, by saunt an' sinner,
How daur ye set your fit upon her,
   Sae fine a *Lady*!
Gae somewhere else and seek your dinner,
   On some poor body.

Swith, in some beggar's haffet squattle;
There ye may creep, and sprawl, and sprattle
Wi' ither kindred, jumping cattle,
   In shoals and nations;
Whare *horn* nor *bane* ne'er daur unsettle
   Your thick plantations.

Now haud you there, ye're out o'sight,
Below the fatt'rels, snug and tight;
Na faith ye yet! ye'll no be right
   Till ye've got on it,
The vera tapmost, tow'ring height
   O' *Miss's* bonnet.

My sooth! right bauld ye set your nose out,
As plump an' gray as onie grozet;
O for some rank, mercurial rozet,
   Or fell, red smeddum,
I'd gie ye sic a hearty dose o't
   Wad dress your droddum!

I wad na been surpris'd to spy
You on an auld wife's *flainen toy*:
Or aiblins some bit duddie boy,
   On's *wylecoat*;
But Miss's fine *Lunardi*! Fye!
   How daur ye do't?

O *Jenny*, dinna toss your head,
An' set your beauties a' abroad!
Ye little ken what cursed speed
     The blastie's makin!
Thae *winks* and *finger-ends*, I dread,
     Are notice takin!

O wad some Pow'r the giftie gie us
To see oursels as others see us!
It wad frae monie a blunder free us
     An' foolish notion:
What airs in dress an' gait wad lea'e us,
     An' ev'n Devotion!

Green grow the Rashes, O

Chorus

Green grow the rashes, O;
Green grow the rashes, O;
The sweetest hours that e'er I spent,
Are spent amang the lasses, O.

There's nought but care on ev'ry han',
In every hour that passes, O:
What signifies the life o' man,
An' 'twere na for the lasses, O.
     Green grow, &c.

The warly race may riches chase,
An' riches still may fly them, O;
An' tho' at last they catch them fast,
Their hearts can ne'er enjoy them, O.
     Green grow, &c.

But gie me a cannie hour at e'en,
My arms about my Dearie, O;
An' warly cares, an' warly men,
May a' gae tapsalteerie, O!
     Green grow, &c.

For you sae douse, ye sneer at this,
Ye're nought but senseless asses, O:
The wisest Man the warl' saw,
He dearly lov'd the lasses, O.
     Green grow, &c.

Auld Nature swears, the lovely Dears
Her noblest work she classes, O:
Her prentice han' she try'd on man,
An' then she made the lasses, O.
Green grow, &c.

Of a' the airts

OR

I love my Jean

Of a' the airts the wind can blaw,
I dearly like the West;
For there the bony Lassie lives,
The Lassie I lo'e best:
There's wild-woods grow, and rivers row,
And mony a hill between;
But day and night my fancy's flight
Is ever wi' my Jean.

I see her in the dewy flowers,
I see her sweet and fair;
I hear her in the tunefu' birds,
I hear her charm the air:
There's not a bony flower, that springs,
By fountain, shaw, or green;
There's not a bony bird that sings
But minds me o' my Jean.

Ae fond kiss

Ae fond kiss, and then we sever;
Ae fareweel and then for ever!
Deep in heart-wrung tears I'll pledge thee,
Warring sighs and groans I'll wage thee.

Who shall say that fortune grieves him
While the star of hope she leaves him?
Me, nae chearfu' twinkle lights me;
Dark despair around benights me.

I'll ne'er blame my partial fancy,
Naething could resist my Nancy:
But to see her, was to love her;
Love but her, and love for ever.
Had we never lov'd sae kindly,
Had we never lov'd sae blindly,
Never met – or never parted,
We had ne'er been broken-hearted.

Fare thee weel, thou first and fairest!
Fare thee weel, thou best and dearest!
Thine be ilka joy and treasure,
Peace, enjoyment, love and pleasure!

Ae fond kiss, and then we sever;
Ae fareweel, Alas! for ever!
Deep in heart-wrung tears I'll pledge thee,
Warring sighs and groans I'll wage thee.

Ca' the yowes to the knowes

Chorus

Ca' the yowes to the knowes,
Ca' them whare the heather growes,
Ca' them whare the burnie rowes,
My bonie dearie.

Hark, the mavis' evening sang
Sounding Clouden's woods amang;
Then a-faulding let us gang,
My bonie dearie.
            Ca' the yowes, &c.

We'll gae down by Clouden side,
Thro' the hazels spreading wide,
O'er the waves, that sweetly glide
To the moon sae clearly.
            Ca' the yowes, &c.

Yonder Clouden's silent towers,
Where at moonshine midnight hours,
O'er the dewy bending flowers,
Fairies dance sae cheary.
            Ca' the yowes, &c.

Ghaist nor bogle shalt thou fear;
Thou'rt to love and heaven sae dear,
Nocht of ill may come thee near,
My bonie dearie.
Ca' the yowes, &c.

Fair and lovely as thou art,
Thou has stown my very heart;
I can die – but canna part,
My bonie dearie.
Ca' the yowes, &c.

A red, red Rose

O, my Luve's like a red, red rose,
That's newly sprung in June,
O, my Luve's like the melodie
That's sweetly play'd in tune.

As fair art thou, my bonie lass,
So deep in luve am I;
And I will love thee still, my Dear,
Till a' the seas gang dry.

Till a' the seas gang dry, my Dear,
And the rocks melt wi' the sun:
I will love thee still, my Dear,
While the sands o' life shall run.

And fare thee weel, my only Luve!
And fare thee weel, a while!
And I will come again, my Luve,
Tho' it were ten thousand mile!

O whistle, and I'll come to you, my lad

O whistle, and I'll come to you, my lad,
O whistle, and I'll come to you, my lad;
Tho' father and mother and a' should gae mad,
O whistle, and I'll come to you, my lad.

But warily tent, when ye come to court me,
And come na unless the back-yett be a-jee;
Syne up the back-style, and let naebody see,

And come, as ye were na coming to me.
And come, as ye were na coming to me.
O whistle, &c.

At kirk, or at market whene'er ye meet me,
Gang by me as tho' that ye car'd nae a flie;
But steal me a blink o' your bonie black e'e,
Yet look as ye were na looking at me,
Yet look as ye were na looking at me.
O whistle, &c.

Ay vow and protest that ye carena for me,
And whyles ye may lightly my beauty a wee;
But court nae anither, tho' joking ye be,
For fear that she wyle your fancy frae me,
For fear that she wyle your fancy frae me.
O whistle, &c.

Tam o' Shanter

A TALE

Of Brownyis and of Bogillis full is this buke.
GAWIN DOUGLAS

When chapman billies leave the street,
And drouthy neebors, neebors meet,
As market-days are wearing late,
An' folk begin to tak the gate;
While we sit bousing at the nappy,
An' getting fou and unco happy,
We think na on the lang Scots miles,
The mosses, waters, slaps, and styles,
That lie between us and our hame,
Whare sits our sulky, sullen dame,
Gathering her brows like gathering storm,
Nursing her wrath to keep it warm.

This truth fand honest *Tam o' Shanter*,
As he frae Ayr ae night did canter,
(Auld Ayr, wham ne'er a town surpasses,
For honest men and bonny lasses.)

O *Tam*! had'st thou but been sae wise,
As ta'en thy ain wife *Kate's* advice!
She tauld thee weel thou was a skellum,

Ae market night

A blethering, blustering, drunken blellum;
That frae November till October,
Ae market-day thou was nae sober;
That ilka melder, wi' the miller,
Thou sat as lang as thou had siller;
That ev'ry naig was ca'ed a shoe on,
The smith and thee got roaring fou on;
That at the Lord's house, even on Sunday,
Thou drank wi' Kirkton Jean till Monday.
She prophesied that, late or soon,
Thou would be found deep drown'd in Doon;
Or catch'd wi' warlocks in the mirk,
By *Alloway's* auld haunted kirk.

Ah, gentle dames! it gars me greet,
To think how mony counsels sweet,
How mony lengthen'd sage advices,
The husband frae the wife despises!

But to our tale: Ae market-night,
Tam had got planted unco right;
Fast by an ingle, bleezing finely,
Wi' reaming swats, that drank divinely;
And at his elbow, Souter *Johnny*,
His ancient, trusty, drouthy crony;
Tam lo'ed him like a vera brither;
They had been fou for weeks thegither.
The night drave on wi' sangs and clatter;
And ay the ale was growing better:
The landlady and *Tam* grew gracious,
Wi' favours, secret, sweet, and precious:
The Souter tauld his queerest stories;
The landlord's laugh was ready chorus:
The storm without might rair and rustle,
Tam did na mind the storm a whistle.

Care, mad to see a man sae happy,
E'en drown'd himsel amang the nappy:
As bees flee hame wi' lades o' treasure,
The minutes wing'd their way wi' pleasure:
Kings may be blest, but *Tam* was glorious,
O'er a' the ills o' life victorious!

But pleasures are like poppies spread,
You seize the flow'r, its bloom is shed;
Or like the snow falls in the river,

A moment white – then melts for ever;
Or like the borealis race,
That flit ere you can point their place;
Or like the rainbow's lovely form
Evanishing amid the storm.
Nae man can tether time or tide;
The hour approaches *Tam* maun ride;
That hour, o' night's black arch the key-stane,
That dreary hour he mounts his beast in;
And sic a night he taks the road in,
As ne'er poor sinner was abroad in.

The wind blew as 'twad blawn its last;
The rattling showers rose on the blast;
The speedy gleams the darkness swallow'd:
Loud, deep, and lang, the thunder bellow'd:
That night, a child might understand,
The Deil had business on his hand.

Weel mounted on his gray mare, *Meg*,
A better never lifted leg,
Tam skelpit on thro' dub and mire,
Despising wind, and rain, and fire;
Whiles holding fast his gude blue bonnet;
Whiles crooning o'er some auld Scots sonnet;
Whiles glowring round wi' prudent cares,
Lest bogles catch him unawares:
Kirk-Alloway was drawing nigh,
Whare ghaists and houlets nightly cry.

By this time he was cross the ford,
Whare, in the snaw, the chapman smoor'd;
And past the birks and meikle stane,
Whare drunken *Charlie* brak's neck-bane;
And thro' the whins, and by the cairn,
Whare hunters fand the murder'd bairn;
And near the thorn, aboon the well,
Whare *Mungo's* mither hang'd hersel.
Before him *Doon* pours all his floods;
The doubling storm roars thro' the woods;
The lightnings flash from pole to pole;
Near and more near the thunders roll:
When, glimmering thro' the groaning trees,
Kirk-Alloway seem'd in a bleeze;
Thro' ilka bore the beams were glancing;
And loud resounded mirth and dancing–.

Inspiring bold *John Barleycorn*!
What dangers thou can make us scorn!
Wi' tippeny, we fear nae evil;
Wi' usquabae, we'll face the devil!
The swats sae ream'd in *Tammie's* noddle,
Fair play, he car'd na deils a boddle.
But *Maggie* stood right sair astonish'd,
Till, by the heel and hand admonish'd,
She ventur'd forward on the light;
And, wow! *Tam* saw an unco sight!
Warlocks and witches in a dance;
Nae cotillion, brent new frae *France*,
But hornpipes, jigs, strathspeys, and reels,
Put life and mettle in their heels.
A winnock-bunker in the east,
There sat auld Nick, in shape o' beast,
A towzie tyke, black, grim, and large,
To gie them music was his charge:
He screw'd the pipes and gart them skirl,
Till roof and rafters a' did dirl.
Coffins stood round, like open presses,
That shaw'd the dead in their last dresses;
And by some devilish cantraip slight
Each in its cauld hand held a light.
By which heroic *Tam* was able
To note upon the haly table,
A murderer's banes in gibbet airns;
Twa span-lang, wee, unchristen'd bairns;
A thief, new-cutted frae a rape,
Wi' his last gasp his gab did gape;
Five tomahawks, wi' blude red-rusted;
Five scymitars, wi' murder crusted;
A garter, which a babe had strangled;
A knife, a father's throat had mangled.
Whom his ain son o' life bereft,
The grey hairs yet stack to the heft;
Wi' mair o' horrible and awefu',
Which even to name wad be unlawfu'.

As *Tammie* glower'd, amaz'd, and curious,
The mirth and fun grew fast and furious:
The piper loud and louder blew;
The dancers quick and quicker flew;
They reel'd, they set, they cross'd, they cleekit,
Till ilka carlin swat and reekit,
And coost her duddies to the wark,
And linket at it in her sark!

Now, *Tam*, O *Tam*! had thae been queans,
A' plump and strapping in their teens,
Their sarks, instead o' creeshie flannen,
Been snaw-white seventeen hunder linnen!
Thir breeks o' mine, my only pair,
That ance were plush, o' gude blue hair,
I wad hae gi'en them off my hurdies,
For ae blink o' the bonie burdies!

But wither'd beldams, auld and droll,
Rigwoodie hags wad spean a foal,
Lowping and flinging on a crummock,
I wonder didna turn thy stomach.

But *Tam* kend what was what fu' brawlie,
There was ae winsome wench and wawlie,
That night enlisted in the core,
(Lang after kend on *Carrick* shore;
For mony a beast to dead she shot,
And perish'd mony a bony boat,
And shook baith meikle corn and bear,
And kept the country-side in fear).
Her cutty sark, o' Paisley harn,
That while a lassie she had worn,
In longitude tho' sorely scanty,
It was her best, and she was vauntie. -
Ah! little kend thy reverend grannie,
That sark she coft for her wee Nannie,
Wi' twa pund Scots ('twas a' her riches),
Wad ever grac'd a dance of witches!

But here my Muse her wing maun cour;
Sic flights are far beyond her pow'r;
To sing how Nannie lap and flang,
(A souple jade she was, and strang),
And how *Tam* stood, like ane bewitch'd,
And thought his very een enrich'd;
Even Satan glowr'd, and fidg'd fu' fain,
And hotch'd and blew wi' might and main;
Till first ae caper, syne anither,
Tam tint his reason a' thegither,
And roars out. 'Weel done, Cutty-sark!'
And in an instant all was dark:
And scarcely had he Maggie rallied,
When out the hellish legion sallied.

As bees bizz out wi' angry fyke,
When plundering herds assail their byke;
As open pussie's mortal foes,
When, pop! she starts before their nose;
As eager runs the market-crowd,
When 'Catch the thief!' resounds aloud;
So Maggie runs, the witches follow,
Wi' mony an eldritch skreech and hollow.

Ah, *Tam*! Ah, *Tam*! thou'll get thy fairin!
In hell they'll roast thee like a herrin!
In vain thy *Kate* awaits thy comin!
Kate soon will be a woefu' woman!
Now, do thy speedy utmost, Meg,
And win the key-stane of the brig;
There at them thou thy tail may toss,
A running stream they dare na cross.
But ere the key-stane she could make,
The fient a tail she had to shake!
For Nannie, far before the rest,
Hard upon noble Maggie prest,
And flew at *Tam* wi' furious ettle;
But little wist she Maggie's mettle —
Ae spring brought off her master hale,
But left behind her ain grey tail:
The carlin claught her by the rump,
And left poor Maggie scarce a stump.

Now, wha this tale o' truth shall read,
Ilk man and mother's son, take heed:
Whene'er to drink you are inclin'd,
Or cutty-sarks run in your mind,
Think, ye may buy the joys o'er dear,
Remember Tam o' Shanter's mare.

Mary Morison

O Mary, at thy window be,
It is the wish'd, the trysted hour;
Those smiles and glances let me see,
That make the miser's treasure poor:
How blythly wad I bide the stoure,
A weary slave frae sun to sun;
Could I the rich reward secure,
The lovely Mary Morison!

Yestreen when to the trembling string,
The dance gaed thro' the lighted ha',
To thee my fancy took its wing,
I sat, but neither heard or saw:
Tho' this was fair, and that was braw,
And yon the toast of a' the town,
I sigh'd, and said amang them a',
'Ye are na Mary Morison.'

O Mary, canst thou wreck his peace,
Wha for thy sake wad gladly die!
Or canst thou break that heart of his,
Whase only faute is loving thee.
If love for love thou wilt na gie,
At least be pity to me shown;
A thought ungentle canna be
The thought o' Mary Morison.

Holy Willie's Prayer

O thou that in the heavens does dwell!
Wha, as it pleases best thysel,
Sends ane to heaven and ten to hell,
    A' for thy glory!
And no for ony gude or ill
    They've done before thee.

I bless and praise thy matchless might,
When thousands thou has left in night,
That I am here before thy sight,
    For gifts and grace,
A burning and a shining light
    To a' this place.

What was I, or my generation,
That I should get such exaltation?
I, wha deserv'd most just damnation,
    For broken laws
Sax thousand years ere my creation,
    Thro' Adam's cause.

When from my mother's womb I fell,
Thou might hae plunged me deep in hell,
To gnash my gooms, and weep, and wail,
      In burning lakes,
Where damned devils roar and yell
      Chain'd to their stakes.

Yet I am here, a chosen sample,
To shew thy grace is great and ample:
I'm here, a pillar o' thy temple
      Strong as a rock,
A guide, a ruler and example
      To a' thy flock.

But yet – O Lord – confess I must
At times I'm fash'd wi' fleshly lust;
And sometimes too, in warldly trust
      Vile Self gets in;
But thou remembers we are dust,
      Defil'd wi' sin.

O Lord–yestreen–thou kens–wi' Meg –
Thy pardon I sincerely beg!
O may't ne'er be a living plague,
      To my dishonor!
And I'll ne'er lift a lawless leg
      Again upon her.

Besides, I farther maun avow,
Wi' Leezie's lass, three times – I trow –
But, Lord, that Friday I was fou
      When I cam near her;
Or else, thou kens, thy servant true
      Wad never steer her.

Maybe thou lets this fleshly thorn
Buffet thy servant e'en and morn,
Lest he o'er proud and high should turn,
      That he's sae gifted;
If sae, thy hand maun e'en be borne
      Untill thou lift it.

Lord bless thy Chosen in this place,
For here thou has a chosen race:
But God, confound their stubborn face,
      And blast their name,

Wha bring thy rulers to disgrace
        And open shame.

Lord mind Gaun Hamilton's deserts!
He drinks, and swears, and plays at cartes,
Yet has sae mony taking arts
        Wi' great and sma',
Frae God's ain priest the people's hearts
        He steals awa.

And when we chasten'd him therefore,
Thou kens how he bred sic a splore,
And set the warld in a roar
        O' laughin at us:
Curse thou his basket and his store,
        Kail and potatoes.

Lord hear my earnest cry and prayer
Against that Presbytry of Ayr!
Thy strong right hand, Lord, make it bare
        Upon their heads!
Lord visit them, and dinna spare,
        For their misdeeds!

O Lord my God, that glib-tongu'd Aiken!
My very heart and flesh are quaking
To think how I sat, sweating, shaking,
        And piss'd wi' dread,
While Auld wi' hingin lip gaed sneaking
        And hid his head!

Lord, in thy day o' vengeance try him!
Lord, visit him that did employ him!
And pass not in thy mercy by them;
        Nor hear their prayer;
But for thy people's sake destroy them,
        And dinna spare!

But Lord; remember me and mine
Wi' mercies temporal and divine!
That I for grace and gear may shine,
        Excell'd by nane!
And a' the glory shall be thine!
        Amen! Amen!

The Twa Dogs

A TALE

'Twas in that place o' *Scotland's* isle,
That bears the name o' auld king Coil,
Upon a bonie day in June,
When wearing thro' the afternoon,
Twa Dogs, that were na thrang at hame,
Forgather'd ance upon a time.

The first I'll name, they ca'd him *Caesar*,
Was keepet for His Honor's pleasure;
His hair, his size, his mouth, his lugs,
Shew'd he was nane o' Scotland's dogs,
But whalpet some place far abroad,
Where sailors gang to fish for Cod.

His locked, letter'd, braw brass-collar
Shew'd him the *gentleman* an' *scholar*;
But tho' he was o' high degree,
The fient a pride na pride had he,
But wad hae spent an hour caressan,
Ev'n wi' a tinkler-gypsey's *messan*:
At *Kirk* or *Market*, *Mill* or *Smiddie*,
Nae tawtied *tyke*, tho' e'er sae duddie,
But he wad stan't, as glad to see him,
An' stroan't on stanes an' hillocks wi' him.

The tither was a *ploughman's collie*,
A rhyming, ranting, raving billie,
Wha for his friend an' comrade had him,
And in his freaks had *Luath* ca'd him,
After some dog in *Highlan sang*,
Was made lang syne, lord knows how lang.

He was a gash, and faithfu' *tyke*,
As ever lap a sheugh or dyke!
His honest, sonsie, baws'nt *face*,
Aye gat him friends in ilka place;
His *breast* was white, his towzie *back*
Weel clad wi' coat o' glossy black;
His gawsie tail, wi' upward curl,
Hung owre his hurdies wi' a swirl.

Nae doubt but they were fain o' ither,
An' unco pack an' thick thegither;

Wi' social *nose* whyles snuff d an' snowcket;
Whyles mice and modewurks they howcket;
Whyles scour'd away in lang excursion,
An' worry'd ither in *diversion*;
Till tir'd at last wi' mony a farce,
They set them down upon their arse,
An' there began a lang digression
About the lords o' the creation.

CAESAR

I've aften wonder'd, honest *Luath*,
What sort o' life poor dogs like you have;
An' when the *gentry's* life I saw,
What way *poor bodies* liv'd ava.

Our *Laird* gets in his racked rents,
His coals, his kane, an a' his stents:
He rises when he likes himsel;
His flunkies answer at the bell;
He ca's his coach; he cals his horse;
He draws a bonie, silken purse
As lang's my tail, whare thro' the steeks,
The yellow, letter'd *Geordie* keeks.

Frae morn to een it's nought but toiling,
At baking, roasting, frying, boiling;
An' tho' the gentry first are steghan,
Yet ev'n the *ha' folk* fill their peghan
Wi' sauce, ragouts, an' sic like trashrie,
That's little short o' downright wastrie.
Our *Whipper-in*, wee blastet wonner,
Poor worthless elf, it eats a dinner,
Better than ony *Tenant-man*
His Honor has in a' the lan':
An' what poor *Cot-folk* pit their painch in,
I own it's past my comprehension.

LUATH

Trowth, *Caesar*, whyles they're fash't enough;
A *Cotter* howckan in a sheugh,
Wi' dirty stanes biggan a dyke,
Bairan a quarry an' sic like,
Himsel, a wife, he thus sustains,
A smytrie o' wee, duddie weans,
An' nought but his han'-daurk, to keep
Them right an' tight in *thack an' raep*.

An' when they meet wi' sair disasters,
Like loss o' health, or want o' masters,
Ye maist wad think, a wee touch langer,
An' they maun starve o' cauld an' hunger:
But how it comes, I never kent yet,
They're maistly wonderfu' contented;
An' buirdly chiels, and clever hizzies,
Are bred in sic a way as this is.

CAESAR

But then, to see how ye're negleket,
How huff'd, an' cuff'd, an' disrespeket!
Lord man, our gentry care as little
For *delvers*, *ditchers*, an' sic cattle;
They gang as saucy by poor folk,
As I wad by a stinkan brock.

I've notic'd on our Laird's *court-day*,
An' mony a time my heart's been wae,
Poor *tenant bodies*, scant o' cash,
How they maun thole a *factor's* snash;
He'll stamp and threaten, curse an' swear,
He'll *apprehend* them, *poind* their gear;
While they maun stan', wi' aspect humble,
An' hear it a', an' fear an' tremble!

I see how folk live that hae riches,
But surely poor folk maun be *wretches*!

LUATH

They're no sae wretched's ane wad think;
Tho' constantly on poortith's brink,
They're sae accustom'd wi' the sight,
The view o't gies them little fright.

Then chance and fortune are sae guided.
They're ay in less or mair provided;
An' tho' fatigu'd wi' close employment,
A blink o' rest's a sweet enjoyment.
The dearest comfort o' their lives,
Their grushie weans an' faithfu' wives;
The *prattling things* are just their pride,
That sweetens a' their fire-side.

An' whyles twalpennie-worth o' *nappy*
Can mak the bodies unco happy;

They lay aside their private cares,
To mind the Kirk and State affairs;
They'll talk o' *patronage* an' *priests*,
Wi' kindling fury i' their breasts,
Or tell what new taxation's comin,
An' ferlie at the folk in Lon'on.

As bleak-fac'd Hallowmass returns,
They get the jovial, rantan *Kirns*,
When *rural* life, of ev'ry station,
Unite in common recreation;
Love blinks, Wit slaps, an' social Mirth
Forgets there's *care* upo' the earth.

That *merry day* the year begins,
They bar the door on frosty win's;
The nappy reeks wi' mantling ream,
An' sheds a heart-inspiring steam;
The luntan pipe, an' sneeshin mill,
Are handed round wi' right guid will;
The cantie, auld folks, crackan crouse,
The young anes rantan thro' the house –
My heart has been sae fain to see them,
That I for joy hae *barket* wi' them.

Still it's owre true that ye hae said,
Sic game is now owre aften play'd;
There's monie a creditable flock
O' decent, honest, fawsont folk,
Are riven out baith root an' branch,
Some rascal's pridefu' greed to quench,
Wha thinks to knit himsel the faster
In favor wi' some *gentle Master*,
Wha, aiblins thrang *a-parliamentin*,
For Britain's guid! his saul indentin-

CAESAR

Haith lad ye little ken about it;
For Britain's guid! guid faith! I doubt it.
Say rather, gaun as Premiers lead him,
An' saying *aye* or *no's* they bid him:
At Operas an' Plays parading,
Mortgaging, gambling, masquerading:
Or maybe, in a frolic daft.
To Hague or Calais takes a waft,
To make a *tour* an' tak a whirl,
To learn *bon ton* and see the worl'.

There, at Vienna or Versailles,
He rives his father's auld entails;
Or by Madrid he takes the rout.
To thrum *guittarres* an' fecht wi' *nowt*;
Or down *Italian Vista* startles,
Whore-hunting amang groves o' myrtles:
Then bowses drumlie *German-water*,
To mak himsel look fair and fatter,
An' clear the consequential sorrows,
Love-gifts of Carnival Signioras.
For Britain's guid! for her destruction!
Wi' dissipation, feud an' faction!

LUATH

Hech man! dear sirs! is that the gate
They waste sae mony a braw estate!
Are we sae foughten and harass'd
For gear to gang that gate at last!

O would they stay aback frae courts,
An' please themsels wi' countra sports,
It wad for ev'ry ane be better,
The *Laird*, the *Tenant*, an' the *Cotter*!
For thae frank, rantan, ramblan billies,
Fient haet o' them's ill hearted fellows;
Except for breakin o' their timmer,
Or speakin lightly o' their *Limmer*,
Or shootin of a hare or moorcock,
The ne'er-a-bit they're ill to poor folk.

But will ye tell me, master *Caesar*,
Sure *great folk's* life's a life o' pleasure?
Nae cauld nor hunger e'er can steer them,
The vera thought o't need na fear them.

CAESAR

Lord man, were ye but whyles where I am,
The *gentles* ye wad ne'er envy them!

It's true, they need na starve or sweat,
Thro' Winter's cauld, or Summer's heat;
They've nae sair-wark to craze their banes,
An' fill *auld-age* wi' grips an' granes;
But *human-bodies* are sic fools,
For a' their Colledges an' Schools,
That when nae *real* ills perplex them,

They *mak* enow themsels to vex them;
An' ay the less they hae to sturt them,
In like proportion, less will hurt them.

A country fellow at the pleugh,
His *acre's* till'd, he's right eneugh;
A country girl at her wheel,
Her *dizzen's* done, she's unco weel;
But Gentlemen, an' Ladies warst,
Wi' ev'n down *want o' wark* are curst.
They loiter, lounging, lank an' lazy;
Tho' deil-haet ails them, yet uneasy;
Their days, insipid, dull an' tasteless,
Their nights, unquiet, lang an' restless.

An' ev'n their sports, their balls an' races,
Their galloping through public places,
There's sic parade, sic pomp an' art,
The joy can scarcely reach the heart.

The *Men* cast out in *party-matches*,
Then sowther a' in deep debauches.
Ae night, they're mad wi' drink an' whuring,
Niest day their life is past enduring.

The *Ladies* arm-in-arm in clusters,
As great an' gracious a' as sisters;
But hear their *absent thoughts* o' ither,
They're a' run-deils an' jads thegither.
Whyles, owre the wee bit cup an' platie,
They sip the *scandal-potion* pretty;
Or lee-lang nights, wi' crabbet leuks,
Pore owre the devil's *pictur'd beuks*;
Stake on a chance a farmer's stackyard,
An' cheat like ony *unhang'd blackguard*.

There's some exceptions, man an' woman;
But this is Gentry's life in common.

By this, the sun was out o' sight,
An' darker gloamin brought the night:
The *bum-clock* humm'd wi' lazy drone,
The kye stood rowtan i' the loan;
When up they gat an' shook their lugs,
Rejoic'd they were na *men* but *dogs*;
An' each took off his several way,
Resolv'd to meet some ither day.

Address to the Unco Guid

OR THE RIGIDLY RIGHTEOUS

My son, these maxims make a rule,
And lump them ay thegither;
The Rigid Righteous *is a fool,*
The Rigid Wise *anither.*
The cleanest corn that e'er was dight
May hae some pyles o' caff in;
So ne'er a fellow-creature slight
For random fits o' daffin.
>   SOLOMON: Eccles. ch. vii, ver. 16

I

O ye wha are sae guid yoursel,
Sae pious and sae holy,
Ye've nought to do but mark and tell
Your Neebours' fauts and folly!
Whase life is like a weel-gaun mill,
Supply'd wi' store o' water,
The heapet happer's ebbing still,
An' still the clap plays clatter.

II

Hear me, ye venerable Core,
As counsel for poor mortals,
That frequent pass douce Wisdom's door
For glaikit Folly's portals;
I, for their thoughtless, careless sakes,
Would here propone defences,
Their donsie tricks, their black mistakes,
Their failings and mischances.

III

Ye see your state wi' theirs compar'd
And shudder at the niffer,
But cast a moment's fair regard,
What makes the mighty differ;
Discount what scant occasion gave,
That purity ye pride in,
And (what's aft mair than a' the lave)
Your better art o' hiding.

IV

Think, when your castigated pulse
Gies now and then a wallop,
What ragings must his veins convulse,
That still eternal gallop:
Wi' wind and tide fair i' your tail,
Right on ye scud your sea-way;
But in the teeth o' baith to sail,
It makes an unco leeway.

V

See Social-life and Glee sit down,
All joyous and unthinking,
Till, quite transmugrify'd, they're grown
Debauchery and Drinking:
O would they stay to calculate
Th' eternal consequences;
Or your more dreaded hell to state,
Damnation of expences!

VI

Ye high, exalted, virtuous Dames,
Ty'd up in godly laces,
Before ye gie poor *Frailty* names,
Suppose a change o' cases;
A dear-lov'd lad, convenience snug,
A treacherous inclination –
But, let me whisper i' your lug,
Ye're aiblins nae temptation.

VII

Then gently scan your brother Man,
Still gentler sister Woman;
Tho' they may gang a kennin wrang,
To step aside is human:
One point must still be greatly dark,
The moving *Why* they do it;
And just as lamely can ye mark,
How far perhaps they rue it.

VIII

Who made the heart, 'tis *He* alone
Decidedly can try us,
He knows each chord its various tone,
Each spring its various bias:
Then at the balance let's be mute,
We never can adjust it;
What's done we partly may compute,
But know not what's resisted.

The birks of Aberfeldy

Chorus

Bonie lassie, will ye go,
Will ye go, will ye go,
Bonie lassie, will ye go
To the birks of Aberfeldy?

Now Simmer blinks on flow'ry braes –
And o'er the crystal streamlets plays;
Come let us spend the lightsome days
In the birks of Aberfeldy.
   Bonie lassie, &c.

The little birdies blythely sing,
While o'er their heads the hazels hing,
Or lightly flit on wanton wing
In the birks of Aberfeldy.
   Bonie lassie, &c.

The braes ascend like lofty wa's,
The foamy stream deep-roaring fa's,
O'erhung wi' fragrant-spreading shaws,
The birks of Aberfeldy.
   Bonie lassie, &c.

The hoary cliffs are crown'd wi' flowers,
White o'er the linns the burnie pours,
And rising weets wi' misty showers
The birks of Aberfeldy.
   Bonie lassie, &c.

Let Fortune's gifts at random flee,
They ne'er shall draw a wish frae me;

Supremely blest wi' love and thee
In the birks of Aberfeldy.
Bonie lassie, &c.

The Jolly Beggars - A Cantata

RECITATIVO

When lyart leaves bestrow the yird,
Or wavering like the Bauckie-bird,
Bedim cauld Boreas' blast;
When hailstanes drive wi' bitter skyte,
And infant frosts begin to bite,
In hoary cranreuch drest;
Ae night at e'en a merry core
O' randie, gangrel bodies,
In Poosie-Nansie's held the splore,
To drink their orra duddies;
Wi' quaffing an' laughing,
They ranted an' they sang,
Wi' jumping an' thumping,
The vera girdle rang.

First, neist the fire, in auld red rags,
Ane sat, weel brac'd wi' mealy bags,
And knapsack a' in order;
His doxy lay within his arm;
Wi' usquebae an' blankets warm
She blinkit on her Sodger;
An' aye he gies the tozie drab
The tither skelpin kiss,
While she held up her greedy gab,
Just like an aumous dish;
Ilk smack still, did crack still,
Just like a cadger's whip;
Then staggering an' swaggering
He roar'd this ditty up –

AIR

Tune: 'Soldier's Joy'

I am a son of Mars who have been in many wars,
And show my cuts and scars wherever I come;

This here was for a wench, and that other in a trench,
When welcoming the French at the sound of the drum.
        Lal de daudle, etc.

My prenticeship I past where my leader breath'd his last,
When the bloody die was cast on the heights of Abram:
And I served out my trade when the gallant game was play'd,
And the Moro low was laid at the sound of the drum.

I lastly was with Curtis among the floating *batt'ries*,
And there I left for witness, an arm and a limb:
Yet let my country need me, with Elliot to head me,
I'd clatter on my stumps at the sound of a drum.

And now tho' I must beg, with a wooden arm and leg,
And many a tatter'd rag hanging over my bum,
I'm as happy with my wallet, my bottle and my Callet,
As when I used in scarlet to follow a drum.

What tho', with hoary locks, I must stand the winter shocks,
Beneath the woods and rocks oftentimes for a home,
When the tother bag I sell, and the tother bottle tell,
I could meet a troop of Hell, at the sound of a drum.

RECITATIVO

He ended; and the kebars sheuk,
Aboon the chorus roar;
While frighted rattons backward leuk,
An' seek the benmost bore:
A fairy fiddler frae the neuk,
He skirl'd out, encore!
But up arose the martial chuck,
An' laid the loud uproar.

AIR

Tune: 'Sodger Laddie'

I once was a maid, tho' I cannot tell when,
And still my delight is in proper young men:
Some one of a troop of dragoons was my daddie,
No wonder I'm fond of a sodger laddie.
        Sing, lal de lal, etc.

The first of my loves was a swaggering blade,
To rattle the thundering drum was his trade;

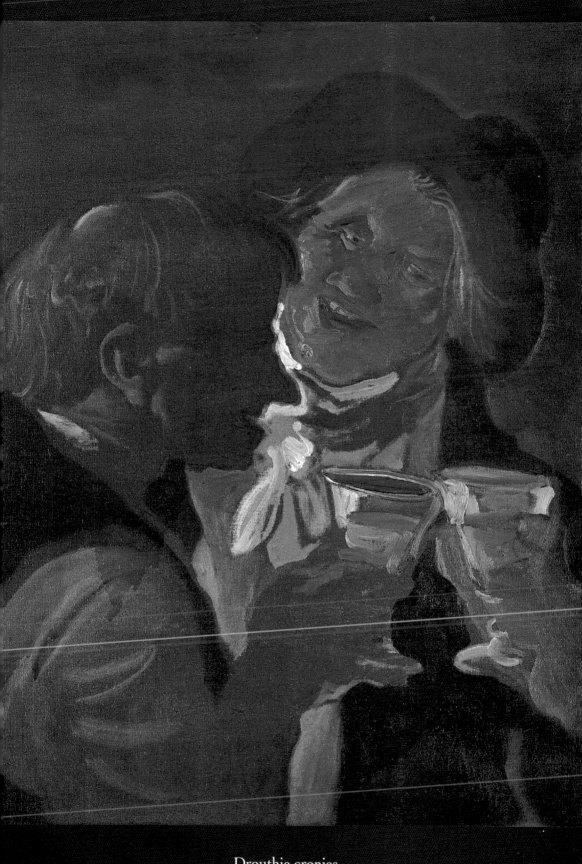

Drouthie cronies

His leg was so tight, and his cheek was so ruddy,
Transported I was with my sodger laddie.

But the godly old chaplain left him in the lurch;
The sword I forsook for the sake of the church:
He ventur'd the soul, and I risked the body,
'Twas then I proved false to my sodger laddie.

Full soon I grew sick of my sanctified *Sot*,
The regiment at large for a husband I got;
From the gilded spontoon to the fife I was ready,
I asked no more but a sodger laddie.

But the peace it reduc'd me to beg in despair,
Till I met my old boy in a Cunningham fair;
His rags regimental, they flutter'd so gaudy,
My heart it rejoic'd at a sodger laddie.

And now I have liv'd – I know not how long,
But still I can join in a cup and a song;
And whilst with both hands I can hold the glass steady,
Here's to thee, my hero, my sodger laddie.

RECITATIVO

Poor Merry-Andrew, in the neuk,
Sat guzzling wi' a tinkler-hizzie;
They mind't na what the chorus teuk,
Between themsels they were sae busy:
At length, wi' drink an' courting dizzy,
He stoiter'd up an' made a face;
Then turn'd an' laid a smack on Grizzie,
Syne tun'd his pipes wi' grave grimace.

AIR

Tune: 'Auld Sir Symon'

Sir Wisdom's a fool when he's fou;
Sir Knave is a fool in a session;
He's there but a prentice I trow,
But I am a fool by profession.

My grannie she bought me a beuk,
An' I held awa to the school;
I fear I my talent misteuk,
But what will ye hae of a fool?

For drink I would venture my neck;
A hizzie's the half of my Craft;
But what could ye other expect
Of ane that's avowedly daft?

I ance was tied up like a stirk,
For civilly swearing and quaffin;
I ance was abus'd i' the kirk,
For towsing a lass i' my daffin.

Poor Andrew that tumbles for sport,
Let naebody name wi' a jeer;
There's even, I'm tauld, i' the Court
A Tumbler ca'd the Premier.

Observ'd ye yon reverend lad
Mak faces to tickle the mob;
He rails at our mountebank squad, —
It's rivalship just i' the job.

And now my conclusion I'll tell,
For faith I'm confoundedly dry;
The chiel that's a fool for himsel',
Guid Lord! he's far dafter than I.

RECITATIVO

The niest out spak a raucle Carlin,
Wha kent fu' weel to cleek the Sterlin;
For monie a pursie she had hooked,
An' had in mony a well been douked:
Her love had been a Highland laddie,
But weary fa' the waeful woodie!
Wi' sighs and sobs she thus began
To wail her braw John Highlandman.

AIR

Tune: 'O an ye were dead, Guidman'

A Highland lad my Love was born,
The Lalland laws he held in scorn;
But he still was faithfu' to his clan,
My gallant, braw John Highlandman

Chorus

Sing hey my braw John Highlandman!
Sing ho my braw John Highlandman!
There's not a lad in a' the lan'
Was match for my John Highlandman.

With his philibeg an' tartan plaid,
An' guid claymore down by his side,
The ladies' hearts he did trepan,
My gallant, braw John Highlandman.
Sing hey, &c.

We ranged a' from Tweed to Spey,
An' liv'd like lords an' ladies gay;
For a Lalland face he feared none, —
My gallant, braw John Highlandman.
Sing hey, &c.

They banish'd him beyond the sea.
But ere the bud was on the tree,
Adown my cheeks the pearls ran,
Embracing my John Highlandman.
Sing hey, &c.

But, och! they catch'd him at the last,
And bound him in a dungeon fast:
My curse upon them every one,
They've hang'd my braw John Highlandman!
Sing hey, &c.

And now a widow, I must mourn
The pleasures that will ne'er return:
No comfort but a hearty can,
When I think on John Highlandman.
Sing hey, &c.

RECITATIVO

A pigmy Scraper wi' his Fiddle,
Wha us'd to trystes an' fairs to driddle,
Her strapping limb and gausy middle
         (He reach'd nae higher)
Had hol'd his heartie like a riddle,
         An' blawn't on fire.

Wi' hand on hainch, and upward e'e,
He croon'd his gamut, one, two, three,

Then in an arioso key,
        The wee Apollo
Set off wi' allegretto glee
        His giga solo.

AIR

Tune: 'Whistle owre the lave o't'

Let me ryke up to dight that tear,
An' go wi' me an' be my dear;
An' then your every care an' fear
May whistle owre the lave o't.

Chorus

I am a fiddler to my trade,
An' a' the tunes that e'er I played,
The sweetest still to wife or maid,
Was whistle owre the lave o't.

At kirns an' weddins we'se be there,
An' O sae nicely's we will fare!
We'll bowse about till Daddie Care
Sing whistle owre the lave o't.
        I am, &c.,

Sae merrily's the banes we'll pyke,
An' sun oursel's about the dyke;
An' at our leisure, when ye like,
We'll whistle owre the lave o't.
        I am, &c.,

But bless me wi' your heav'n o' charms,
An' while I kittle hair on thairms,
Hunger, cauld, an' a' sic harms,
May whistle owre the lave o't.
        I am, &c.,

RECITATIVO

Her charms had struck a sturdy caird,
As weel as poor gut-scraper;
He taks the Fiddler by the beard,
An' draws a roosty rapier—
He swoor by a' was swearing worth,
To speet him like a Pliver,

Unless he would from that time forth
Relinquish her for ever:

Wi' ghastly e'e, poor tweedle-dee
Upon his hunkers bended,
An' pray'd for grace wi' ruefu' face,
An' so the quarrel ended.
But tho' his little heart did grieve
When round the tinkler prest her,
He feign'd to snirtle in his sleeve,
When thus the caird address'd her:

AIR

Tune: 'Clout the Cauldron'

My bonie lass, I work in brass,
A tinkler is my station:
I've travell'd round all Christian ground
In this my occupation;
I've ta'en the gold, an' been enrolled
In many a noble squadron;
But vain they search'd when off I march'd
To go an' clout the cauldron.
                I've ta'en the gold, &c.,

Despise that shrimp, that wither'd imp,
With a' his noise an' cap'rin;
An take a share wi' those that bear
The *budget* and the *apron*!
And by that stowp, my faith an' houp,
And by that dear Kilbaigie,
If e'er ye want, or meet wi' scant,
May I ne'er weet my craigie.
                And by that stowp, &c.,

RECITATIVO

The caird prevail'd — th' unblushing fair
In his embraces sunk;
Partly wi' love o'ercome sae sair,
An' partly she was drunk:
Sir Violino, with an air
That show'd a man o' spunk,
Wish'd unison between the pair,
An' made the bottle clunk
        To their health that night.

But hurchin Cupid shot a shaft,
That play'd a dame a shavie—
The fiddler rak'd her, fore and aft,
Behint the chicken cavie.
Her lord, a wight of Homer's craft,
Tho' limpin wi' the spavie,
He hirpl'd up, an' lap like daft,
An' shor'd them Dainty Davie
      O' boot that night.

He was a care-defying blade
As ever Bacchus listed!
Tho' Fortune sair upon him laid,
His heart, she ever miss'd it.
He had no wish but—to be glad,
Nor want but—when he thristed;
He hated nought but—to be sad,
An' thus the muse suggested
      His sang that night.

AIR

Tune: 'For a' that, an' a' that'

I am a Bard of no regard,
Wi' gentle folks an' a' that;
But Homer-like, the glowrin byke,
Frae town to town I draw that.

Chorus

For a' that, an' a' that,
An' twice as muckle's a' that;
I've lost but ane, I've twa behin',
I've wife eneugh for a' that.

I never drank the Muses' stank,
Castalia's burn, an' a' that;
But there it streams an' richly reams,
My Helicon I ca' that.
    For a' that, &c.,

Great love I bear to a' the fair,
Their humble slave an' a' that;
But lordly Will, I hold it still
A mortal sin to thraw that.
    For a' that, &c.,

In raptures sweet, this hour we meet,
Wi' mutual love an' a' that;
But for how lang the flie may stang,
Let inclination law that.
        For a' that, &c.,

Their tricks an' craft hae put me daft,
They've taen me in, an' a' that;
But clear your decks, and here's—'The Sex!'
I like the jads for a' that.

Chorus

For a' that, an' a' that,
An' twice as muckle's a' that;
My dearest bluid, to do them guid,
They're welcome till't for a' that.

RECITATIVO

So sang the bard—and Nansie's wa's
Shook with a thunder of applause,
Re-echo'd from each mouth!
They toom'd their pocks, they pawn'd their duds,
They scarcely left to co'er their fuds,
To quench their lowin drouth:
Then owre again, the jovial thrang
The poet did request
To lowse his pack an' wale a sang,
A ballad o' the best;
He rising, rejoicing,
Between his twa Deborahs,
Looks round him, an' found them
Impatient for the chorus.

AIR

Tune: 'Jolly Mortals, fill your Glasses'

See the smoking bowl before us,
Mark our jovial ragged ring!
Round and round take up the chorus,
And in raptures let us sing—

Chorus

A fig for those by law protected!
Liberty's a glorious feast!
Courts for cowards were erected,
Churches built to please the priest.

What is title, what is treasure,
What is reputation's care?
If we lead a life of pleasure,
'Tis no matter how or where!
       A fig for, &c.,

With the ready trick and fable,
Round we wander all the day;
And at night in barn or stable,
Hug our doxies on the hay.
       A fig for, &c.,

Does the train-attended carriage
Thro' the country lighter rove?
Does the sober bed of marriage
Witness brighter scenes of love?
       A fig for, &c.,

Life is all a variorum,
We regard not how it goes;
Let them cant about decorum,
Who have character to lose.
       A fig for, &c.,

Here's to budgets, bags and wallets!
Here's to all the wandering train.
Here's our ragged brats and callets,
One and all cry out, Amen!

Chorus

A fig for those by law protected!
Liberty's a glorious feast!
Courts for cowards were erected,
Churches built to please the priest.

No Churchman am I

No Churchman am I for to rail and to write,
No Statesman nor Soldier to plot or to fight,
No sly man of business contriving a snare,
For a big-belly'd bottle's the whole of my care.

The Peer I don't envy, I give him his bow;
I scorn not the Peasant, tho' ever so low;
But a club of good fellows, like those that are there,
And a bottle like this, are my glory and care.

Here passes the Squire on his brother—his horse;
There Centum per Centum, the Cit with his purse;
But see you the Crown how it waves in the air,
There a big-belly'd bottle still eases my care.

The wife of my bosom, alas! she did die;
For sweet consolation to church I did fly;
I found that old Solomon proved it fair,
That a big-belly'd bottle's a cure for all care.

I once was persuaded a venture to make;
A letter inform'd me that all was to wreck;
But the pursy old landlord just waddl'd up stairs,
With a glorious bottle that ended my cares.

'Life's cares they are comforts'—a maxim laid down
By the Bard, what d'ye call him, that wore the black gown;
And faith I agree with th' old prig to a hair;
For a big-belly'd bottle's a heav'n of care.

A Stanza added in a Mason Lodge

Then fill up a bumper and make it o'erflow,
And honours masonic prepare for to throw;
May ev'ry true Brother of th' Compass and Square
Have a big-belly'd bottle when harass'd with care.

Address to a Haggis

Fair fa' your honest, sonsie face,
Great Chieftain o' the Puddin-race!
Aboon them a' ye tak your place,
    Painch, tripe, or thairm:
Weel are ye wordy of a *grace*
    As lang's my arm.

The groaning trencher there ye fill,
Your hurdies like a distant hill,
Your *pin* wad help to mend a mill
    In time o' need,
While thro' your pores the dews distil
    Like amber bead.

His knife see Rustic-labour dight,
An' cut you up wi' ready slight,
Trenching your gushing entrails bright
    Like onie ditch;
And then, O what a glorious sight,
    Warm-reekin, rich!

Then, horn for horn they stretch an' strive,
Deil tak the hindmost, on they drive,
Till a' their weel-swall'd kytes belyve
    Are bent like drums;
Then auld Guidman, maist like to rive,
    Bethankit hums.

Is there that owre his French *ragout*,
Or *olio* that wad staw a sow,
Or *fricassee* wad mak her spew
    Wi' perfect sconner
Looks down wi' sneering, scornfu' view
    On sic a dinner?

Poor devil! see him owre his trash,
As feckless as a wither'd rash,
His spindle shank a guid whip-lash,
    His nieve a nit;
Thro' bluidy flood or field to dash,
    O how unfit!

But mark the Rustic, *haggis-fed*,
The trembling earth resounds his tread,

Clap in his walie nieve a blade,
        He'll mak it whissle;
An' legs, an' arms, an' heads will sned,
        Like taps o' thrissle.

Ye Pow'rs wha mak mankind your care,
And dish them out their bill o' fare,
Auld Scotland wants nae skinking ware,
        That jaups in luggies;
But, if ye wish her gratefu' prayer,
        Gie her a *Haggis*!

The Deil's awa wi' th' Exciseman

The deil cam fiddlin thro' the town,
And danc'd awa wi' th' Exciseman;
And ilka wife cries, auld Mahoun,
I wish you luck o' the prize, man.

Chorus

The deil's awa, the deil's awa
The deil's awa wi' th' Exciseman,
He's danc'd awa, he's danc'd awa
He's danc'd awa wi' th' Exciseman.

We'll mak our maut and we'll brew our drink,
We'll laugh, sing, and rejoice, man;
And mony braw thanks to the meikle black deil,
That danc'd awa wi' th' Exciseman.
        The deil's awa, &c.

There's threesome reels, there's foursome reels,
There's hornpipes and strathspeys, man,
But the ae best dance e'er cam to the Land
Was, the deil's awa wi' th' Exciseman.
        The deil's awa, &c.

My Bonie Mary

Go, fetch to me a pint o' wine,
And fill it in a silver tassie,
That I may drink, before I go,
A service to my bonie lassie:
The boat rocks at the Pier o' Leith,
Fu' loud the wind blaws frae the Ferry;

The ship rides by the Berwick-law,
And I maun leave my bonie Mary.
The trumpets sound, the banners fly,
The glittering spears are ranked ready,
The shouts o' war are heard afar,
The battle closes deep and bloody.
It's not the roar o' sea or shore,
Wad make me langer wish to tarry;
Nor shouts o' war thus heard afar, —
It's leaving thee, my bonie Mary!

The Captain's Lady

Chorus

O mount and go,
Mount and make you ready;
O mount and go,
And be the Captain's Lady.

When the drums do beat,
And the cannons rattle;
Thou shalt sit in state,
And see thy love in battle.
O mount, &c

When the vanquish'd foe
Sues for peace and quiet;
To the shades we'll go,
And in love enjoy it.
O mount, &c.

Logan Water

O Logan, sweetly didst thou glide,
That day I was my Willie's bride,
And years sinsyne hae o'er us run,
Like Logan to the simmer sun;
But now thy flowery banks appear
Like drumlie Winter, dark and drear;
While my dear lad maun face his faes,
Far, far frae me and Logan braes.

Again the merry month o' May,
Has made our hills and valleys gay;
The birds rejoice in leafy bowers,

The bees hum round the breathing flowers:
Blythe Morning lifts his rosy eye,
And Evening's tears are tears of joy:
My soul, delightless, a' surveys,
While Willie's far frae Logan braes.

Within yon milk-white hawthorn bush,
Amang her nestlings sits the thrush;
Her faithfu' mate will share her toil,
Or wi' his song her cares beguile:
But I wi' my sweet nurslings here—
Nae mate to help, nae mate to cheer,
Pass widow'd nights and joyless days,
While Willie's far frae Logan braes.

O wae upon you, Men o' State,
That brethren rouse in deadly hate!
As ye make mony a fond heart mourn,
Sae may it on your heads return!
How can your flinty hearts enjoy
The widow's tears, the orphan's cry?
But soon may peace bring happy days,
And Willie, hame to Logan braes!

For a' that and a' that

Is there, for honest Poverty
That hings his head, and a' that?
The coward-slave, we pass him by—
We dare be poor for a' that!
For a' that, and a' that,
Our toils obscure, and a' that,
The rank is but the guinea's stamp,
The man's the gowd for a' that.

What though on hamely fare we dine,
Wear hoddin grey, and a' that?
Gie fools their silks, and knaves their wine,
A Man's a Man, for a' that:
For a' that, and a' that,
Their tinsel show, and a' that;
The honest man, though e'er sae poor,
Is king o' men for a' that.

Ye see yon birkie ca'd, a lord,
Wha struts, and stares, and a' that;
Though hundreds worship at his word,
He's but a coof for a' that:
For a' that, and a' that,
His ribband, star, and a' that;
The man of independent mind,
He looks and laughs at a' that.

A prince can mak' a belted knight,
A marquis, duke, and a' that;
But an honest man's aboon his might,
Gude faith he mauna fa' that!
For a' that, and a' that,
Their dignities, and a' that;
The pith o' Sense, and pride o' Worth,
Are higher rank than a' that.

Then let us pray that come it may,
As come it will for a' that,
That Sense and Worth, o'er a' the earth,
May bear the gree, and a' that:
For a' that, and a' that,
It's comin' yet for a' that,
That Man to Man, the warld o'er,
Shall brothers be for a' that!

Scots wha hae wi' Wallace bled

Scots, wha hae wi' Wallace bled,
Scots, wham Bruce has aften led,
Welcome to your gory bed,
  Or to victory!

Now's the day, and now's the hour;
See the front o' battle lour:
See approach proud Edward's power —
  Chains and slavery!

Wha will be a traitor knave?
Wha can fill a coward's grave?
Wha sae base as be a Slave?
  Let him turn and flee!

Wha for Scotland's king and law
Freedom's sword will strongly draw?
Freeman stand, or Freeman fa'?
      Let him follow me.

By Oppression's woes and pains!
By your Sons in servile chains!
We will drain our dearest veins,
      But they shall be free!

Lay the proud Usurpers low!
Tyrants fall in every foe!
Liberty's in every blow! —
      Let us do or die!

Such a parcel of rogues in a nation

Fareweel to a' our Scottish fame,
Fareweel our ancient glory;
Fareweel ev'n to the Scottish name,
Sae fam'd in martial story!
Now Sark rins over Solway sands,
An' Tweed rins to the ocean,
To mark where England's province stands,
Such a parcel of rogues in a nation!

What force or guile could not subdue,
Thro' many warlike ages,
Is wrought now by a coward few,
For hireling traitor's wages.
The English steel we could disdain,
Secure in valour's station;
But English gold has been our bane,
Such a parcel of rogues in a nation!

O would, or I had seen the day
That Treason thus could sell us,
My auld grey head had lien in clay
Wi' Bruce and loyal Wallace!
But pith and power, till my last hour
I'll mak this declaration;
We're bought and sold for English gold,
Such a parcel of rogues in a nation!

Bonie wee thing

Chorus

Bonie wee thing, cannie wee thing,
Lovely wee thing, wert thou mine,
I would wear thee in my bosom,
Lest my jewel I should tine

Wishfully I look and languish,
In that bonie face of thine;
And my heart it stounds wi' anguish,
Lest my wee thing be na mine.
Bonie wee, &c

Wit, and Grace, and Love, and Beauty,
In ae constellation shine;
To adore thee is my duty,
Goddess o' this soul o' mine!
Bonie wee, &c

Charlie, he's my darling

'Twas on a Monday morning,
Right early in the year,
That Charlie came to our town —
The young Chevalier.

Chorus

An' Charlie, he's my darling,
My darling, my darling;
Charlie, he's my darling —
The young Chevalier.

As he was walking up the street,
The city for to view;
O there he spied a bonie lass
The window looking thro'.
An' Charlie, &c.

Sae light's he jimped up the stair,
And tirled at the pin;
And wha sae ready as hersel'
To let the laddie in?
An' Charlie, &c.

Doon pours all his floods

He set his Jenny on his knee,
All in his Highland dress;
For brawlie weel he ken'd the way
To please a bonie lass.
An' Charlie, &c.

It's up yon heathery mountain,
And down yon scroggy glen,
We daurna gang a-milking
For Charlie and his men!
An' Charlie, &c.

Comin' thro' the rye

Comin' thro' the rye, poor body,
Comin' thro' the rye;
She draigl't a' her petticoatie,
Comin' thro' the rye.

Chorus

Oh, Jenny's a' weet, poor body,
Jenny's seldom dry;
She draigl't a' her petticoatie,
Comin' thro' the rye.

Gin a body meet a body
Comin' thro' the rye;
Gin a body kiss a body,
Need a body cry?
Oh, Jenny's a' weet, &c.

Gin a body meet a body
Comin' thro' the glen;
Gin a body kiss a body,
Need the warld ken?
Oh, Jenny's a' weet, &c.

Killiecrankie

Whare hae ye been sae braw, lad?
Whare hae ye been sae brankie, O?
Whare hae ye been sae braw, lad?
Cam ye by Killiecrankie, O?

Chorus

An ye had been whare I hae been,
Ye wad na been sae canty, O;
An ye had seen what I hae seen,
On th' braes o' Killiecrankie, O.

I faught at land, I faught at sea;
At hame I faught my auntie, O;
But I met the Devil and Dundee,
On th' braes o' Killiecrankie, O.
   An ye had been, &c.

The bauld Pitcur fell in a furr,
An' Clavers gat a clankie, O;
Or I had fed an Athole gled,'
On th' braes o' Killiecrankie, O.
   An ye had been, &c.

McPherson's Farewell

Farewell, ye dungeons dark and strong,
The wretch's destinie!
McPherson's time will not be long,
On yonder gallows-tree.

Chorus

Sae rantingly, sae wantonly,
Sae dauntonly gae'd he:
He play'd a spring, and danc'd it round,
Below the gallows-tree.

O what is death but parting breath?
On many a bloody plain
I've dar'd his face, and in this place
I scorn him yet again!
   Sae rantingly, &c.

Untie these bands from off my hands,
And bring to me my sword;
And there's no a man in all Scotland,
But I'll brave him at a word.
            Sae rantingly, &c.

I've liv'd a life of sturt and strife;
I die by treacherie:
It burns my heart I must depart,
And not avenged be.
            Sae rantingly, &c.

Now farewell light, thou sunshine bright,
And all beneath the sky!
May coward shame distain his name,
The wretch that dares not die!
            Sae rantingly, &c.

At Inveraray

Whoe'er he be that sojourns here,
I pity much his case,
Unless he come to wait upon
The Lord their God, his Grace.

There's naething here but Highland pride,
And Highland scab and hunger;
If Providence has sent me here,
'Twas surely in an anger.

Lines written on a bank-note

Wae worth thy power, thou cursed leaf!
Fell source of a' my woe and grief!
For lack o' thee I've lost my lass,
For lack o' thee I scrimp my glass:
I see the children of affliction,
Unaided, through thy curs'd restriction;
I've seen th' Oppressor's cruel smile,
Amid his hapless victim's spoil,
And for thy potence vainly wisht,
To crush the Villain in the dust!
For lack o' thee, I leave this much-lov'd shore,
Never perhaps to greet old Scotland more!

The Farewell

Farewell, old Scotia's bleak domains,
Far dearer than the torrid plains
Where rich ananas blow!
Farewell, a mother's blessing dear!
A brother's sigh! a sister's tear!
My Jean's heart-rending throe!
Farewell, my Bess! tho' thou'rt bereft
Of my parental care,
A faithful brother I have left,
My part in him thou'lt share:
Adieu too, to you too,
My Smith, my bosom frien';
When kindly you mind me,
O then befriend my Jean!
What bursting anguish tears my heart!
From thee, my Jeany, must I part!
Thou, weeping, answ'rest – 'No!'
Alas! misfortune stares my face,
And points to ruin and disgrace,
I for thy sake must go!
Thee, Hamilton, and Aiken dear,
A grateful, warm adieu!
I, with a much indebted tear,
Shall still remember you!
All-hail then, the gale then,
Wafts me from thee, dear shore!
It rustles, and whistles
I'll never see thee more!

Address to the Toothache

My curse upon your venom'd stang,
That shoots my tortur'd gums alang;
And through my lugs gies mony a twang,
        Wi' gnawing vengeance;
Tearing my nerves wi' bitter pang,
        Like racking engines!

When fevers burn, or ague freezes,
Rheumatics gnaw, or cholic squeezes;

Our neighbour's sympathy may ease us,
     Wi' pitying moan;
But thee—thou hell o' a' diseases,
     Aye mocks our groan!

A' down my beard the slavers trickle!
I throw the wee stools o'er the mickle,
As round the fire the giglets keckle,
     To see me loup;
While raving mad, I wish a heckle
     Were in their doup!

O' a' the num'rous human dools,
     Ill har'sts, daft bargains, *cutty-stools*,
Or worthy friends rak'd i' the mools,
     Sad sight to see!
The tricks o' knaves, or fash o' fools—
     Thou bear'st the gree.

Where'er that place be priests ca' hell,
Whence a' the tones o' mis'ry yell,
And ranked plagues their numbers tell,
     In dreadfu' raw,
Thou, TOOTHACHE, surely bear'st the bell
     Amang them a'!

O thou grim mischief-making chiel',
That gars the notes of *discord* squeel,
'Till daft mankind aft dance a reel
     In gore a shoe-thick;—
Gie a' the faes o' SCOTLAND'S weal
     A towmond's Toothache

Lines under the Portrait of Fergusson

Curse on ungrateful man, that can be pleas'd,
And yet can starve the author of the pleasure!

O thou my elder brother in misfortune,
By far my elder brother in the muse,
With tears I pity thy unhappy fate!
Why is the bard unfitted for the world,
Yet has so keen a relish of its pleasures?

The Humble Petition of Bruar Water

TO THE NOBLE DUKE OF ATHOLE

My Lord, I know, your noble ear
Woe ne'er assails in vain;
Embolden'd thus, I beg you'll hear
Your humble slave complain,
How saucy Phoebus' scorching beams,
In flaming summer-pride,
Dry-withering, waste my foamy streams,
And drink my crystal tide.

The lightly-jumping, glowrin' trouts,
That thro' my waters play,
If, in their random, wanton spouts,
They near the margin stray;
If, hapless chance! they linger lang,
I'm scorching up so shallow,
They're left the whitening stanes among,
In gasping death to wallow.

Last day I grat wi' spite and teen,
As Poet B**** came by,
That, to a Bard, I should be seen
Wi' half my channel dry:
A panegyric rhyme, I ween,
Even as I was he shor'd me;
But, had I in my glory been,
He, kneeling, wad ador'd me.

Here, foaming down the skelvy rocks,
In twisting strength I rin;
There, high my boiling torrent smokes,
 Wild-roaring o'er a linn:
Enjoying large each spring and well
As Nature gave them me,
I am, altho' I say't mysel',
Worth gaun a mile to see.

Would then my noble master please
To grant my highest wishes,
He'll shade my banks wi' towering trees,
And bonie spreading bushes.
Delighted doubly then, my Lord,
You'll wander on my banks,

And listen mony a grateful bird
Return you tuneful thanks.

The sober laverock, warbling wild,
Shall to the skies aspire;
The gowdspink, Music's gayest child,
Shall sweetly join the choir:
The blackbird strong, the lintwhite clear,
The mavis mild and mellow;
The robin pensive Autumn chear,
In all her locks of yellow.

This too, a covert shall ensure,
To shield them from the storm;
And coward maukin sleep secure,
Low in her grassy form:
Here shall the shepherd make his seat,
To weave his crown of flowers;
Or find a sheltering, safe retreat,
From prone-descending showers.

And here, by sweet endearing stealth,
Shall meet the loving pair,
Despising worlds with all their wealth
As empty idle care:
The flowers shall vie in all their charms
The hour of heaven to grace,
And birks extend their fragrant arms
To screen the dear embrace.

Here haply too, at vernal dawn,
Some musing bard may stray,
And eye the smoking, dewy lawn,
And misty mountain, grey;
Or, by the reaper's nightly beam,
Mild-chequering thro' the trees,
Rave to my darkly-dashing stream,
Hoarse-swelling on the breeze.

Let lofty firs, and ashes cool,
My lowly banks o'erspread,
And view, deep-bending in the pool,
Their shadows' wat'ry bed:
Let fragrant birks, in woodbines drest,
My craggy cliffs adorn;
And, for the little songster's nest,
The close embowering thorn.

So may Old Scotia's darling hope,
Your little angel band,
Spring, like their fathers, up to prop
Their honour'd, native land!
So may, thro' Albion's farthest kin,
To social-flowing glasses,
The grace be — 'Athole's honest men,
And Athole's bonie lasses!'

My Nanie, O

Behind yon hills where Lugar flows,
'Mang moors an' mosses many, O,
The wintry sun the day has clos'd,
And I'll awa to Nanie, O.

The westlin wind blaws loud an' shill;
The night's baith mirk and rainy, O;
But I'll get my plaid an' out I'll steal,
An' owre the hill to Nanie, O.

My Nanie's charming, sweet an' young;
Nae artfu' wiles to win ye, O:
May ill befa' the flattering tongue
That wad beguile my Nanie, O.

Her face is fair, her heart is true,
As spotless as she's bonie, O;
The op'ning gowan, wat wi' dew,
Nae purer is than Nanie, O.

A country lad is my degree,
An' few there be that ken me, O;
But what care I how few they be,
I'm welcome ay to Nanie, O.

My riches a's my penny-fee,
An' I maun guide it cannie, O;
But warl's gear ne'er troubles me,
My thoughts are a', my Nanie, O.

Our auld Guidman delights to view
His sheep an' kye thrive bonie, O;
But I'm as blythe that hauds his pleugh,
An' has nae care but Nanie, O.

Come weel come woe, I care na by,
I'll tak what Heav'n will sen' me, O;
Nae ither care in life have I,
But live, an' love my Nanie, O.

Address to Edinburgh

Edina! *Scotia's* darling seat!
All hail thy palaces and tow'rs,
Where once beneath a Monarch's feet
Sat Legislation's sov'reign pow'rs!
From marking wildly-scatt'red flow'rs,
As on the banks of *Ayr* I stray'd,
And singing, lone, the ling'ring hours,
I shelter in thy honor'd shade.

Here Wealth still swells the golden tide,
As busy Trade his labours plies;
There Architecture's noble pride
Bids elegance and splendor rise;
Here Justice, from her native skies,
High wields her balance and her rod;
There Learning, with his eagle eyes,
Seeks Science in her coy abode.

Thy Sons, *Edina*, social, kind.
With open arms the Stranger hail;
Their views enlarg'd, their lib'ral mind,
Above the narrow, rural vale:
Attentive still to Sorrow's wail,
Or modest Merit's silent claim;
And never may their sources fail!
And never envy blot their name!

Thy Daughters bright thy walks adorn,
Gay as the gilded summer sky,
Sweet as the dewy, milk-white thorn,
Dear as the raptur'd thrill of joy!
Fair B—strikes th' adoring eye,
Heav'n's beauties on my fancy shine;
I see the *Sire of Love* on high,
And own his work indeed divine!

There, watching high the least alarms,
Thy rough, rude Fortress gleams afar;
Like some bold Vet'ran, gray in arms,
And mark'd with many a seamy scar:
The pond'rous wall and massy bar,
Grim-rising o'er the rugged rock,
Have oft withstood assailing War,
And oft repell'd th' Invader's shock.

With awe-struck thought, and pitying tears,
I view that noble, stately Dome,
Where *Scotia's* kings of other years,
Fam'd heroes! had their royal home:
Alas, how chang'd the times to come!
Their royal Name low in the dust!
Their hapless Race wild-wand'ring roam!
Tho' rigid Law cries out, 'twas just!

Wild-beats my heart, to trace your steps,
Whose ancestors, in days of yore,
Thro' hostile ranks and ruin'd gaps
Old *Scotia's* bloody lion bore:
Ev'n *I* who sing in rustic lore,
Haply *my Sires* have left their shed,
And fac'd grim Danger's loudest roar,
Bold-following where your Fathers led!

Edina! Scotia's darling seat!
All hail thy palaces and tow'rs,
Where once, beneath a Monarch's feet,
Sat Legislation's sov'reign pow'rs!
From marking wildly-scatt'red flow'rs,
As on the banks of *Ayr* I stray'd,
And singing, lone, the ling'ring hours,
I shelter in thy honor'd shade.

The Book-worms

Through and through the inspired leaves,
Ye maggots make your windings;
But, oh! respect his lordship's taste,
And spare his golden bindings.

Warlocks and witches in a dance

To a Mountain-Daisy

ON TURNING ONE DOWN WITH THE PLOUGH, IN APRIL—1786

Wee, modest, crimson-tipped flow'r,
Thou's met me in an evil hour;
For I maun crush amang the stoure
          Thy slender stem:
To spare thee now is past my pow'r,
          Thou bonie gem.

Alas! it's no thy neebor sweet,
The bonie *Lark*, companion meet!
Bending thee 'mang the dewy weet!
          Wi's spreckl'd breast,
When upward-springing, blythe, to greet
          The purpling East.

Cauld blew the bitter-biting *North*
Upon thy early, humble birth;
Yet chearfully thou glinted forth
          Amid the storm,
Scarce rear'd above the *Parent-earth*
          Thy tender form.

The flaunting *flow'rs* our Gardens yield,
High-shelt'ring woods and wa's maun shield,
But thou, beneath the random bield
          O' clod or stane,
Adorns the histie *stibble-feld*,
          Unseen, alane.

There, in thy scanty mantle clad,
Thy snawie bosom sun-ward spread,
Thou lifts thy unassuming head
          In humble guise;
But now the *share* uptears thy bed,
          And low thou lies!

Such is the fate of artless Maid,
Sweet *flow'ret* of the rural shade!
By Love's simplicity betray'd,
          And guileless trust,
Till she, like thee, all soil'd, is laid
          Low i' the dust.

Such is the fate of simple Bard,
On Life's rough ocean luckless starr'd!
Unskilful he to note the card
      Of *prudent Lore*,
Till billows rage, and gales blow hard,
      And whelm him o'er!

Such fate to *suffering worth* is giv'n,
Who long with wants and woes has striv'n,
By human pride or cunning driv'n
      To Mis'ry's brink,
Till wrench'd of ev'ry stay but HEAV'N,
      He, ruin'd, sink!

Ev'n thou who mourn'st the *Daisy's* fate,
That fate is thing – no distant date;
Stern Ruin's *plough-share* drives, elate,
      Full on thy bloom,
Till crush'd beneath the *furrow's* weight,
      Shall be thy doom!

For the Author's Father

O ye whose cheek the tear of pity stains,
Draw near with pious rev'rence and attend!
Here lie the loving Husband's dear remains,
The tender Father, and the gen'rous Friend.

The pitying Heart that felt for human Woe;
The dauntless heart that fear'd no human Pride;
The Friend of Man, to vice alone a foe;
'For ev'n his failings lean'd to Virtue's side.'

Man was made to Mourn

A DIRGE

When chill November's surly blast
Made fields and forests bare,
One ev'ning, as I wand'red forth,
Along the banks of AIRE,
I spy'd a man, whose aged step
Seem'd weary, worn with care;

His face was furrow'd o'er with years,
And hoary was his hair.

Young stranger, whither wand'rest thou?
Began the rev'rend Sage;
Does thirst of wealth thy step constrain,
Or youthful Pleasure's rage?
Or haply, prest with cares and woes,
Too soon thou hast began,
To wander forth, with me, to mourn
The miseries of Man.

The Sun that overhangs yon moors,
Out-spreading far and wide,
Where hundreds labour to support
A haughty lordling's pride;
I've seen yon weary winter-sun
Twice forty times return;
And ev'ry time has added proofs,
That Man was made to mourn.

O Man! while in thy early years,
How prodigal of time!
Mis-spending all thy precious hours,
Thy glorious, youthful prime!
Alternate Follies take the sway;
Licentious Passions burn;
Which tenfold force gives Nature's law,
That Man was made to mourn.

Look not alone on youthful Prime,
Or Manhood's active might;
Man then is useful to his kind,
Supported is his right:
But see him on the edge of life,
With Cares and Sorrows worn,
Then Age and Want, Oh! ill-match'd pair!
Show Man was made to mourn.

A few seem favourites of Fate,
In Pleasure's lap carest;
Yet, think not all the Rich and Great,
Are likewise truly blest.
But Oh! what crowds in ev'ry land,
All wretched and forlorn,
Thro' weary life this lesson learn,
That Man was made to mourn!

Many and sharp the num'rous Ills
Inwoven with our frame!
More pointed still we make ourselves,
Regret, Remorse and Shame!
And Man, whose heav'n-erected face,
The smiles of love adorn,
Man's inhumanity to Man
Makes countless thousands mourn!

See, yonder poor, o'erlabour'd wight,
So abject, mean and vile,
Who begs a brother of the earth
To give him leave to toil;
And see his lordly *fellow-worm*,
The poor petition spurn,
Unmindful, tho' a weeping wife,
And helpless offspring mourn.

If I'm design'd yon lordling's slave,
By Nature's law design'd,
Why was an independent wish
E'er planted in my mind?
If not, why am I subject to
His cruelty, or scorn?
Or why has Man the will and pow'r
To make his fellow mourn?

Yet, let not this too much, my Son,
Disturb thy youthful breast:
This partial view of human-kind
Is surely not the *last*!
The poor, oppressed, honest man
Had never, sure, been born,
Had there not been some recompense
To comfort those that mourn!

O Death! the poor man's dearest friend,
The kindest and the best!
Welcome the hour, my aged limbs
Are laid with thee at rest!
The Great, the Wealthy fear thy blow,
From pomp and pleasure torn;
But Oh! a blest relief for those
That weary-laden mourn!

A Highland Welcome

When Death's dark stream I ferry o'er
(A time that surely shall come),
In Heaven itself I'll ask no more
Than just a Highland welcome.

Epistle to Davie, a Brother Poet

While winds frae off BEN-LOMOND blaw,
And bar the doors wi' driving snaw,
And hing us owre the ingle,
I set me down, to pass the time,
And spin a verse or twa o' rhyme,
In hamely, *westlin* jingle.
While frosty winds blaw in the drift,
Ben to the chimla lug,
I grudge a wee the *Great-folk's* gift,
That live sae bien an' snug:
I tent less, and want less
Their roomy fire-side;
But hanker, and canker,
To see their cursed pride.

It's hardly in a body's pow'r,
To keep, at times, frae being sour,
To see how things are shar'd;
How *best o' chiels* are whyles in want,
While *Coofs* on countless thousands rant,
And ken na how to wair't:
But DAVIE lad, ne'er fash your head,
Tho' we hae little gear,
We're fit to win our daily bread,
As lang's we're hale and fier:
'Mair spier na, nor fear na,'
Auld age ne'er mind a feg;
The last o't, the warst o't,
Is only but to beg.

To lye in kilns and barns at e'en,
When banes are craz'd, and bluid is thin,
Is, doubtless, great distress!
Yet then *content* could make us blest;
Ev'n then, sometimes we'd snatch a taste
Of truest happiness.

The honest heart that's free frae a'
Intended fraud or guile,
However Fortune kick the ba',
Has ay some cause to smile:
And mind still, you'll find still,
A comfort this nae sma';
Nae mair then, we'll care then,
Nae *farther* we can *fa'*.

What tho', like Commoners of air,
We wander out, we know not where,
But either house or hal'?
Yet *Nature's* charms, the hills and woods,
The sweeping vales, and foaming floods,
Are free alike to all.
In days when Daisies deck the ground,
And Blackbirds whistle clear,
With honest joy, our hearts will bound,
To see the *coming* year:
On braes when we please then,
We'll sit and *sowth* a tune;
Syne *rhyme* till't, we'll time till't,
And sing't when we hae done.

It's no in titles nor in rank;
It's no in wealth like *Lon'on Bank*,
To purchase peace and rest;
It's no in makin muckle, *mair*:
It's no in books; it's no in Lear,
To make us truly blest:
If Happiness hae not her seat
And center in the breast,
We may be *wise*, or *rich*, or *great*,
But never can be *blest*:
Nae treasures, nor pleasures
Could make us happy lang;
The *heart* ay's the part ay,
That makes us right or wrang.

Think ye, that sic as *you* and I,
Wha drudge and drive thro' wet and dry,
Wi' never-ceasing toil;
Think ye, are we less blest than they,
Wha scarcely tent us in their way,
As hardly worth their while?
Alas! how aft, in haughty mood,

GOD'S creatures they oppress!
Or else, neglecting a' that's guid,
They riot in excess!
Baith careless, and fearless,
Of either Heaven or Hell;
Esteeming, and deeming,
It a' an idle tale!

Then let us chearfu' acquiesce;
Nor make our scanty Pleasures less,
By pining at our state:
And, ev'n should Misfortunes come,
I, here wha sit, hae met wi' some,
An's thankfu' for them yet.
They gie the wit of *Age to Youth*;
They let us ken oursel;
They make us see the naked truth,
The *real* guid and ill.
Tho' losses, and crosses,
Be lessons right severe,
There's *wit* there, ye'll get there,
Ye'll find nae other where.

But tent me, DAVIE, *Ace o' Hearts!*
(To say aught less wad wrang the *cartes*,
And flatt'ry I detest)
This life has joys for you and I;
And joys that riches ne'er could buy;
And joys the very best.
There's a' the *Pleasures o' the Heart*,
The *Lover* and the *Frien';*
Ye hae your MEG, your dearest part,
And I my darling JEAN!
It warms me, it charms me,
To mention but her *name*:
It heats me, it beets me,
And sets me a' on flame!

O, all ye *Pow'rs* who rule above!
O THOU, whose very self art *love!*
THOU know'st my words sincere!
The *life blood* streaming thro' my heart,
Or my more dear *Immortal part*,
Is not more fondly dear!
When heart-corroding care and grief
Deprive my soul of rest,

Her dear idea brings relief,
And solace to my breast.
Thou BEING, Allseeing,
O hear my fervent pray'r!
Still take her, and make her,
THY most peculiar care!

All hail! ye tender feelings dear!
The smile of love, the friendly tear,
The sympathetic glow!
Long since, this world's thorny ways
Had number'd out my weary days,
Had it not been for you!
Fate still has blest me with a friend,
In ev'ry care and ill;
And oft a more *endearing* band,
A *tye* more tender still.
It lightens, it brightens,
The tenebrific scene,
To meet with, and greet with,
My DAVIE or my JEAN!

O, how that *name* inspires my style!
The words come skelpan, rank and file,
Amaist before I ken!
The ready measure rins as fine,
As *Phoebus*, and the famous *Nine*
Were glowran owre my pen.
My spavet *Pegasus* will limp,
Till ance he's fairly het;
And then he'll hilch, and stilt, and jimp,
And rin an unco fit:
But least then, the beast then,
Should rue this hasty ride,
I'll light now, and dight now,
His sweaty, wizen'd hide.

The Cotter's Saturday Night

INSCRIBED TO R. A****, ESQ.*

*Robert Aiken, writer in Ayr, one of the poet's early friends and patrons.

My lov'd, my honor'd, much respected friend,
No mercenary Bard his homage pays;
With honest pride I scorn each selfish end,
My dearest meed, a friend's esteem and praise:
To you I sing, in simple Scottish lays,
The *lowly train* in life's sequester'd scene;
The native feelings strong, the guileless ways,
What A**** in a *Cottage* would have been;
Ah! tho' his worth unknown, far happier there I ween!

November chill blaws loud wi' angry sugh;
The short'ning winter-day is near a close;
The miry beasts retreating frae the pleugh;
The black'ning trains o' craws to their repose:
The toil-worn COTTER frae his labor goes,
This night his weekly moil is at an end,
Collects his *spade*, his *mattocks* and his *hoes*,
Hoping the *morn* in ease and rest to spend,
And weary, o'er the moor, his course does hameward bend.

At length his lonely *Cot* appears in view,
Beneath the shelter of an aged tree;
Th' expectant wee-things, toddlan, stacher thro'
To meet their *Dad*, wi' flichterin noise and glee.
His wee-bit ingle, blinkan bonilie,
His clean hearth-stane, his thrifty *Wifie's* smile,
The *lisping infant*, prattling on his knee,
Does a' his weary kiaugh and care beguile,
And makes him quite forget his labor and his toil.

Belyve, the *elder bairns* come drapping in,
At *Service* out, amang the Farmers roun';
Some ca' the pleugh, some herd, some tentie rin
A cannie errand to a neebor town:
Their eldest hope, their *Jenny*, woman-grown,
In youthfu' bloom, Love sparkling in her e'e,
Comes hame, perhaps, to shew a braw new gown,
Or deposite her sair-won penny-fee,
To help her *Parents* dear, if they in hardship be.

With joy unfeign'd, *brothers* and *sisters* meet,
And each for other's weelfare kindly spiers:
The social hours, swift-wing'd, unnotic'd fleet;
Each tells the uncos that he sees or hears,
The *Parents partial* eye their hopeful years;
Anticipation forward points the view;
The *Mother*, wi' her needle an' her sheers,
Gars auld claes look amaist as weel's the new;
The *Father* mixes a', wi' admonition due.

Their Master's and their Mistress's command,
The *youngkers* a' are warned to obey;
And mind their labors wi' an eydent hand,
And ne'er, tho' out o' sight, to jauk or play:
'And O! be sure to fear the LORD alway!
'And mind your *duty*, duely, morn and night!
'Lest in temptation's path ye gang astray,
'Implore his *counsel* and assisting *might*;
'They never sought in vain that sought the LORD aright.'

But hark! a rap comes gently to the door;
Jenny, wha kens the meaning o' the same,
Tells how a neebor lad came o'er the moor,
To do some errands, and convoy her hame.
The wily Mother sees the *conscious flame*
Sparkle in *Jenny's* e'e, and flush her cheek,
With heart-struck, anxious care enquires his name,
While *Jenny* hafflins is afraid to speak;
Weel-pleas'd the Mother hears, it's nae wild, worthless *Rake*.

With kindly welcome, *Jenny* brings him ben;
A *strappan youth*; he takes the Mother's eye;
Blythe *Jenny* sees the *visit's* no ill taen;
The Father cracks of horses, pleughs and kye.
The *youngster's* artless heart o'erflows wi' joy,
But blate and laithfu', scarce can weel behave;
The Mother, wi a woman's wiles, can spy
What makes the *youth* sae bashfu' and sae grave;
Weel-pleas'd to think her *bairn's* respected like the lave.

O happy love! where love like this is found!
O heart-felt raptures! bliss beyond compare!
I've paced much this weary, *mortal round*,
And sage EXPERIENCE bids me this declare —
'If Heaven a draught of heavenly pleasure spare,
'One *cordial* in this melancholy *Vale*,

'Tis when a youthful, loving, *modest* Pair,
'In other's arms, breathe out the tender tale,
'Beneath the milk-white thorn that scents the ev'ning gale.'

Is there in human form, that bears a heart—
A Wretch! a Villain! lost to love and truth!
That can, with studied, sly, ensnaring art,
Betray sweet Jenny's unsuspecting youth?
Curse on his perjur'd arts! dissembling smooth!
Are *Honor, Virtue, Conscience,* all exil'd!
Is there no Pity, no relenting Ruth,
Points to the Parents fondling o'er their Child?
Then paints the *ruin'd Maid,* and their distraction wild!

But now the Supper crowns their simple board,
The healsome *Porritch,* chief of SCOTIA's food:
The soupe their *only Hawkie* does afford,
That 'yont the hallan snugly chows her cood:
The *Dame* brings forth, in complimental mood,
To grace the lad, her weel-hain'd kebbuck, fell,
And aft he's prest, and aft he ca's it guid;
The frugal *Wifie,* garrulous, will tell,
How 'twas a towmond auld, sin' Lint was i' the bell.

The chearfu' Supper done, wi' serious face,
They, round the ingle, form a circle wide;
The Sire turns o'er, with patriarchal grace,
The big *ha'-Bible,* ance his *Father's* pride:
His bonnet rev'rently is laid aside,
His *lyart haffets* wearing thin and bare;
Those strains that once did sweet in ZION glide,
He wales a portion with judicious care;
'*And let us worship GOD!*' he says with solemn air.

They chant their artless notes in simple guise;
They tune their *hearts,* by far the noblest aim:
Perhaps *Dundee's* wild warbling measures rise,
Or plaintive *Martyrs,* worthy of the name;
Or noble *Elgin* beets the heaven-ward flame,
The sweetest far of SCOTIA's holy lays.
Compar'd with these, *Italian trills* are tame;
The tickl'd ears no heart-felt raptures raise;
Nae unison hae they, with our CREATOR's praise.

The priest-like Father reads the sacred page,
How *Abram* was the Friend of GOD on high;

Or, *Moses* bade eternal warfare wage,
With *Amalek's* ungracious progeny;
Or how the *royal Bard* did groaning lye,
Beneath the stroke of Heaven's avenging ire;
Or *Job's* pathetic plaint, and wailing cry;
Or rapt *Isaiah's* wild, seraphic fire;
Or other *Holy Seers* that tune the *sacred lyre*.

Perhaps the *Christian Volume* is the theme,
How *guiltless blood* for *guilty man* was shed;
How HE, who bore in heaven the second name,
Had not on Earth whereon to lay His head:
How His first *followers* and *servants* sped;
The *Precepts sage* they wrote to many a land:
How *he*, who lone in *Patmos* banished,
Saw in the sun a mighty angel stand;
And heard great *Bab'lon's* doom pronounc'd by Heaven's command.

Then kneeling down to HEAVEN'S ETERNAL KING,
The *Saint*, the *Father*, and the *Husband* prays:
Hope 'springs exulting on triumphant wing,'
That *thus* they all shall meet in future days:
There, ever bask in *uncreated rays*,
No more to sigh, or shed the bitter tear,
Together hymning their CREATOR'S praise,
In *such society*, yet still more dear;
While circling Time moves round in an eternal sphere.

Compar'd with *this*, how poor Religion's pride,
In all the pomp of *method*, and of *art*,
When men display to congregations wide,
Devotion's ev'ry grace, except the *heart!*
The POWER, incens'd, the Pageant will desert,
The pompous strain, the sacerdotal stole;
But haply, in some *Cottage* far apart,
May hear, well pleas'd, the language of the *Soul*;
And in His *Book of Life* the Inmates poor enroll.

Then homeward all take off their sev'ral way;
The youngling *Cottagers* retire to rest;
The Parent-pair their *secret homage* pay,
And proffer up to Heaven the warm request,
That 'HE who stills the *raven's* clam'rous nest,
'And decks the *lily* fair in flow'ry pride,
'Would, in the way His *Wisdom* sees the best,
'For *them* and for their *little ones* provide;
'But chiefly, in their hearts with *Grace divine* preside.'

From scenes like these, old SCOTIA's grandeur springs,
That makes her lov'd at home, rever'd abroad:
Princes and lords are but the breath of kings,
'An honest man's the noblest work of GOD:'
And *certes*, in fair Virtue's heavenly road,
The *Cottage* leaves the *Palace* far behind:
What is a lordling's pomp? a cumbrous load,
Disguising oft the *wretch* of human kind,
Studied in arts of Hell, in wickedness refin'd!

O SCOTIA! my dear, my native soil!
For whom my warmest wish to heaven is sent!
Long may thy hardy sons of *rustic toil*,
Be blest with health, and peace, and sweet content!
And O may Heaven their simple lives prevent
From *Luxury's* contagion, weak and vile!
Then howe'er *crowns* and *coronets* be rent,
A *virtuous Populace* may rise the while,
And stand a wall of fire around their much-lov'd ISLE.

O THOU! who pour'd the *patriotic tide*,
That stream'd through Wallace's undaunted heart;
Who dar'd to, nobly, stem tyrannic pride,
Or *nobly die*, the second glorious part:
(The Patriot's GOD, peculiarly thou art,
His *friend, inspirer, guardian* and *reward*!)
O never, never SCOTIA's realm desert,
But still the *Patriot*, and the *Patriot-Bard*,
In bright succession raise, her *Ornament* and *Guard*!

Afton Water

Flow gently, sweet Afton, among thy green braes,
Flow gently, I'll sing thee a song in thy praise;
My Mary's asleep by thy murmuring stream,
Flow gently, sweet Afton, disturb not her dream.

Thou stock-dove whose echo resounds thro' the glen,
Ye wild whistling blackbirds in yon thorny den,
Thou green-crested lapwing thy screaming forbear,
I charge you disturb not my slumbering fair.

How lofty, sweet Afton, thy neighbouring hills,
Far mark'd with the courses of clear, winding rills;
There daily I wander as noon rises high,
My flocks and my Mary's sweet cot in my eye.

How pleasant thy banks and green valleys below,
Where wild in the woodlands the primroses blow;
There oft as mild ev'ning weeps over the lea,
The sweet scented birk shades my Mary and me.

Thy crystal stream, Afton, how lovely it glides,
And winds by the cot where my Mary resides;
How wanton thy waters her snowy feet lave,
As gathering sweet flowerets she stems thy clear wave.

Flow gently, sweet Afton, among thy green braes,
Flow gently, sweet river, the theme of my lays;
My Mary's asleep by thy murmuring stream,
Flow gently, sweet Afton, disturb not her dream.

My heart's in the Highlands

My heart's in the Highlands, my heart is not here,
My heart's in the Highlands a chasing the deer;
Chasing the wild deer, and following the roe:
My heart's in the Highlands, wherever I go.

Farewell to the Highlands, farewell to the North;
The birth place of Valour, the country of Worth:
Wherever I wander, wherever I rove,
The hills of the Highlands for ever I love.

Farewell to the mountains high cover'd with snow;
Farewell to the straths and green valleys below;
Farewell to the forests and wild-hanging woods;
Farewell to the torrents and loud-pouring floods.

My heart's in the Highlands, my heart is not here,
My heart's in the Highlands a-chasing the deer;
Chasing the wild deer, and following the roe;
My heart's in the Highlands, wherever I go.

The Auld Farmer's New-year-morning Salutation to his Auld Mare, Maggie

ON GIVING HER THE ACCUSTOMED RIPP OF
CORN TO HANSEL IN THE NEW-YEAR

A *Guid New-year* I wish you Maggie!
Hae, there's a ripp to thy auld baggie;
Tho' thou's howe-backet, now, an' knaggie,
      I've seen the day,
Thou could hae gaen like ony staggie
        Out owre the lay.

Tho' now thou's dowie, stiff an' crazy,
An' thy auld hide as white's a daisie,
I've seen thee dappl't, sleek an' glaizie,
      A bonie gray:
He should been tight that daur't to *raize* thee,
      Ance in a day.

Thou ance was i' the foremost rank,
A *filly* buirdly, steeve an' swank,
An' set weel down a shapely shank,
      As e'er tread yird;
An' could hae flown out owre a stank,
      Like onie bird.

It's now some nine-an'-twenty-year,
Sin' thou was my *Guidfather's Meere*;
He gied me thee, o' tocher clear,
      An' fifty mark;
Tho' it was sma', 'twas weel-won gear,
      An' thou was stark.

When first I gaed to woo my *Jenny*,
Ye then was trottan wi' your Minnie:
Tho' ye was trickie, slee an' funnie,
      Ye ne'er was donsie;
But hamely, tawie, quiet an' cannie,
      An' unco sonsie.

That *day*, ye pranc'd wi' muckle pride,
When ye bure hame my bonie *Bride*:
An' sweet an' gracefu' she did ride
      Wi' maiden air!
KYLE-STEWART I could bragged wide,
      For sic a *pair*.

Tho' now ye dow but hoyte and hoble,
An' wintle like a saumont-coble,
That day, ye was a jinker noble,
      For heels an' win'!
An' ran them till they a' did wauble,
      Far, far behin'!

When thou an' I were young an' skiegh,
An' *Stable-meals* at Fairs were driegh,
How thou wad prance, an' snore, an' scriegh,
      An' tak the road!
Towns-bodies ran an' stood abiegh,
      An' ca't thee mad.

When thou was corn't, an' I was mellow,
We took the road ay like a Swallow:
At *Brooses* thou had ne'er a fellow,
      For pith an' speed;
But ev'ry tail thou pay't them hollow,
      Whare'er thou gaed.

The sma', droop-rumpl't, hunter cattle,
Might aiblins waur't thee for a brattle;
But *sax Scotch miles*, thou try't their mettle,
      An' gart them whaizle:
Nae whip nor spur, but just a wattle
      O' saugh or hazle.

Thou was a noble *Fittie-lan'*,
As e'er in tug or tow was drawn!
Aft thee an' I, in aught hours gaun,
      On guid March-weather,
Hae turn'd *sax rood* beside our han',
      For days thegither.

Thou never braing't, an' fetch't, an' flisket,
But thy *auld tail* thou wad hae whisket,
An' spread abreed thy weel-fill'd *brisket*,
      Wi' pith an' pow'r,
Till sprittie knowes wad rair't an' risket,
      An' slypet owre.

When frosts lay lang, an' snaws were deep,
An' threaten'd *labor* back to keep,
I gied thy *cog* a wee-bit heap
  Aboon the timmer;
I ken'd my *Maggie* wad no sleep
  For that, or Simmer.

In *cart* or *car* thou never reestet;
The steyest brae thou wad hae fac't it;
Thou never lap, an' sten't, an' breastet,
  Then stood to blaw;
But just thy step a wee thing hastet,
  Thou snoov't awa.

My Pleugh is now thy *bairn-time* a';
Four gallant brutes, as e'er did draw;
Forby sax mae, I've sell't awa,
  That thou hast nurst:
They drew me thretten pund an' twa,
  The vera warst.

Monie a sair daurk we twa hae wrought,
An' wi' the weary warl' fought!
An' monie an *anxious day*, I thought
  We wad be beat!
Yet here to *crazy Age* we're brought,
  Wi' something yet.

An' think na, my auld, trusty *Servan'*,
That now perhaps thou's less deservin,
An' thy *auld days* may end in starvin',
  For my last fow,
A heapet *Stimpart*, I'll reserve ane
  Laid by for you.

We've worn to crazy years thegither;
We'll toyte about wi' ane anither;
Wi' tentie care I'll flit thy tether,
  To some hain'd rig,
Whare ye may nobly rax your leather,
  Wi' sma' fatigue.

The Lass o' Ballochmyle

'Twas even—the dewy fields were green,
On every blade the pearls hang;
The Zephyr wantoned round the bean,
And bore its fragrant sweets alang:
In every glen the mavis sang,
All nature list'ning seem'd the while;
Except where green-wood echoes rang
Amang the braes o' Ballochmyle.

With careless step I onward stray'd,
My heart rejoic'd in nature's joy;
When musing in a lonely glade,
A maiden fair I chanced to spy:
Her look was like the morning's eye,
Her air like nature's vernal smile,
Perfection whispered passing by,
'Behold the lass o' Ballochmyle!'

Fair is the morn in flowery May,
And sweet is night in Autumn mild
When roving thro' the garden gay,
Or wandering in the lonely wild:
But woman, nature's darling child!
There all her charms she does compile;
Even there her other works are foil'd
By the bonie lass o' Ballochmyle!

O had she been a country maid,
And I the happy country swain;
'Tho' sheltered in the lowest shed
That ever rose on Scotland's plain,
Thro' weary winter's wind and rain
With joy, with rapture, I would toil,
And nightly to my bosom strain
The bonie lass o' Ballochmyle.

Then pride might climb the slipp'ry steep;
Where fame and honours lofty shine;
And thirst of gold might tempt the deep,
Or downward seek the Indian mine:
Give me the cot below the pine,
To tend the flocks or till the soil,
And every day have joys divine,
With the bonie lass o' Ballochmyle!

Auld Lang Syne

Should auld acquaintance be forgot
And never brought to mind?
Should auld acquaintance be forgot,
And auld lang syne!

Chorus

For auld lang syne, my dear,
For auld lang syne,
We'll tak a cup o' kindness yet
For auld lang syne.

And surely ye'll be your pint stowp!
And surely I'll be mine!
And we'll tak a cup o' kindness yet,
For auld lang syne.
For auld lang syne, &c.,

We twa hae run about the braes,
And pou'd the gowans fine;
But we've wander'd mony a weary fitt,
Sin auld lang syne.
For auld lang syne, &c.,

We twa hae paidl'd in the burn,
Frae morning sun till dine;
But seas between us braid hae roar'd,
Sin auld lang syne.
For auld lang syne, &c.,

And there's a hand, my trusty fiere!
And gie's a hand o' thine!
And we'll tak a right gude-willie waught,
For auld lang syne.
For auld lang syne, &c.,

In hell they'll roast thee like a herrin'

Burns Sketches
by
Neil Munro

Introduction
by
Brian D. Osborne

— ◆ —

Neil Munro on Robert Burns

Neil Munro (1863-1930), a leading Scottish novelist, short-story writer, influential critic and journalist of the early 20th century, had, like many Scottish writers before and since, a deep interest in the works of Robert Burns. In Munro's case this interest is perhaps more remarkable as he came from a Gaelic-speaking background in Argyll and most of his writing reflected Highland life. Indeed the themes of his major historical novels such as *John Splendid* and *The New Road* are the, often painful, working-out of the process of change in and around his native Loch Fyne. The life and poetry of a lowland, Scots-speaking poet like Burns might have seemed marginal to Munro's cultural background and artistic pre-occupations. However, the power of Burns's writing and the universality of Burns's appeal obviously had its effect on Munro as it has had on writers and artists the world over.

Munro celebrated Burns in *The Immortal Memory*, a poem written in 1894, and which is printed here for the first time since then; analysed him in a thoughtful address to a Burns Supper at the Greenock Burns Club (of which he was Honorary President); and above all pictured him in the four short stories based on scenes from the Ayrshire poet's life which are presented in this volume.

Some of these pieces first made their appearance in Munro's weekly column *The Looker-On* in the *Glasgow Evening News*, but they were added to in 1910 when Munro was commissioned by the publishing house of A & C Black to work with the talented Ayrshire-born artist George Houston (1869-1947) on a colour-plate book devoted to Ayrshire landscape and characters. Munro and Houston were already friends; both were members of the Glasgow Art Club with a variety of common interests. Munro swiftly found that although the publisher's original concept was for an artistic itinerary of Ayrshire he had little aptitude for writing anything like guide-book material and, as he said, "wandered off into story-telling instead." He wrote ten "Idylls" which, in truth, bore very little relation to the Houston colour plates, and were not much more closely related to Houston's black and white sketches which appeared at the beginning and end of each "Idyll."

A reviewer in the *Glasgow Herald*, welcoming the publication of *Ayrshire Idylls*, observed that:

> ... the writer and the artist were not intent on gathering archaeo-
> logical and topographical detail, after the manner of industrious
> delvers; their purpose was to express the character and tempera-
> ment of the county, to reveal something of its soul.

Munro's approach to the soul of Ayrshire was to write about some of the county's people rather than simply describe its topography. In fact, this technique did allow quite a strong feeling for the landscape to come through as a by-product.

Munro's tales depict Ayrshire's most famous son, Robert Burns, at four stages in his career and, quite apart from their intrinsic literary merits and their insight into Burns, are significant as being among the earliest fictional treatments of Burns's life.

Mossgiel Rab, set around 1784, finds the young poet as joint tenant, with his brother Gilbert, of Mossgiel Farm, near Mauchline. Burns is kicking against the restrictions of the farmer's life, condemned to struggle with poor land and a harsh climate, seeking refuge in the conviviality of Poosie Nancy's Inn.

Burns and Clarinda is set in Edinburgh in December 1787. Burns had published the Kilmarnock Edition of his poems in the previous year and had become the darling of literary Edinburgh. It was at this time that he met Agnes Maclehose, with whom he was to conduct the long correspondence with himself in the romantic persona of Sylvander and Mrs Maclehose as Clarinda. It was for "Clarinda" that Burns wrote one of his most affecting love songs *Ae Fond Kiss*.

The third idyll, *The Making of Tam o' Shanter* is a fascinating study of the process of artistic creation, set at Burns's later farm of Ellisland, near Dumfries, in November 1790 with Burns married to the long-suffering Jean Armour. There is a particular poignancy in Burns, removed from his native and much-loved Ayrshire, composing this tale of supernatural spirits and an all too natural man, perhaps the most essentially Ayrshire of all his poems,

> ...he had nothing learned that was not his already when he walked
> behind the plough, and all the fervours, all the sweet illusions and
> enchantments which he gave a voice in song were harvested in
> Ayrshire.

The final piece, *The Democrat*, has Burns in the last phase of his short life, as a gauger (an exciseman), walking the lonely streets of Dumfries, an unpopular supporter of the French Revolution. Burns's support for Revolutionary France, which continued until the French Republic declared war on Britain in January 1793, was hardly politic for a civil servant dependent on official favour for his post and dependent on the income from it to supplement his meagre earnings from Ellisland Farm to feed and clothe his growing family.

Munro's depictions of Burns at four periods of his life and at four phases of his artistic development are interesting and perceptive and make one wish that he had been able to write a more extended piece of fiction based on the life of the poet. There is surely a particular fascination in the insights which one artist brings to describing the work of an earlier artist.

Munro's texts stand securely enough by themselves to be enjoyable and neatly crafted miniatures and his regular publisher, Blackwood, reprinted the collection in 1923 in a "text-only" version. Munro himself thought well of the book, even though he said that he had mainly taken on the contract as a gesture of friendship to Houston, indeed he wrote to G W Blackwood of these stories, "I must add that I think some of them are as good as I've done."

Brian D. Osborne

Former Honorary Publications Officer,
Scottish Library Association.

Neil Munro
The Immortal Memory
Published pseudonymously in the Glasgow Evening News
25th January 1894

Cauld Janwar' win', ye hanselled in
Dear Rab, auld Scotland's bard,
And, by my sang, it wad be wrang
To ca' ye dour and hard.
Yer braggart roar, yer hail and hoar,
We'll tak' in right guid part:
Ye blew ower Ayr when first beat there
Oor bardie's gentle heart.

Had Simmer breeze, 'mang Southron trees,
Its warmth owre Rabbie flung,
We dinna ken but aiblins then
His sang had ne'er been sung:
Or else his lay had been gey wae,
And little worth, a tune
O' jasmine floo'ers and dallying oors,
Or maunderin's 'bout the mune!

For Scotland stern dear Rab was born,
No' for some saft Sooth land,
That puirtith cauld and pride sae bauld
Thegether, couldna' understand.
His harp, sae clear, for Scottish ear
Was tuned on nature's key;
He plucked the strings and gave the wings
To mair than mortal harmony.

The ruined hoose o' shiverin' moose
Brought his saft heart a pang;
The humblest floo'er amang the stour
Was worth his boniest sang.
We feel the fire o' War's desire
Quick lichted by his lay,
Or lauch wi' joy at simple ploy,
Tauld in his pawkie way.

Ae single glass aroon' we'll pass
(Be't either wine or water;
Sae lang's the heart is in the part
It disna' muckle matter).
Confusion to the blackguard crew
That fain wad black his fame!
May guid luck fa'on each an' a'
Wha still upholds his name!

Mossgiel Rab

GILBERT, in his shirt-sleeves, read a book – 'The Life of Hannibal' – more to improve that douce mind of his than for amusement, seemingly, since he yawned at the turning of every page; and Blane, the ploughboy, mended harness. A north wind whooped in the spacious chimney, where a pot hung boiling low on the swee, and the trees, that sheltered Mossgiel steading, cried piteously as for entrance, rapping at the white-harled gable.

On such nights, Gilbert's brother felt, more poignantly than usual, his passion for the wild, his fierce impatience with the humdrum tenor of their peasant home. It was the fire that mainly lit the kitchen; a tallow candle guttering on the brace but gave to the wholesome glow of peat a wan complexion, a hint of the artificial, and to the poet a discontented thought of other chambers read about or seen through unshuttered windows momentarily, where numberless candles shone against sconces on the walls of the well-to-do. He cast a curious glance about him as he sat in a swither with his fingers on the laces of his shoes – at the low, stained rafters, the planked enclosures of the beds, the dresser of chipped blue delf, the sleeping collie, the bubbling pot, the studious brother, the industrious Blane; and the thought in his bosom came to his lips with no restraining – "Gibbie! is this – is this, can ye tell me, our eternal doom?"

Gilbert straightened his stooped back, and turned his fire-freckled face on Robert.

"What's the time?" said he.

Burns drew a watch from the fob of his breeches, glanced at the dial, snapped the words " half-nine," and strode to the pot that swung on the chimney chain. He lifted the lid, peered at the contents – to-morrow's dinner—and shut them from his view again with an iron clatter.

"Offal!" said he. "Is that Hannibal yet ye're at? Was he fed, Gibbie, do you think, on offal?"

"I would ca' nae guid meat offal, Rab," said Gilbert. "And if it had been offal at Capua it wad hae been better for Hannibal and his men. Half-nine? It's time we were bedded".

The eyes of Burns fired deeply under their cliff of brow, the flambeaux of revolt; he grimaced and shrugged his shoulders. "Half-nine," said he, "and bed! What's in the veins o' ye, Gib? – is't buttermilk? In mine thank God! it's blood. I'm for nae stupor on a caff mattress in a loft at half-nine on a nicht like this so lang's there's men to be met at Poosie Nancy's. Here's you and General Hannibal, every line of him wide awake and thrang wi' tramping sodgers, and ye're ganting for your bed, and here's Jock Blane cobbling brechams, content himsel' in the trams o' the dung-cart o' destiny – a kind o' patient cuddy! Please yersels, but I'm neither for bed nor brechams! Three-score years and ten's the allotted span; I misdoubt I'll see but the half o't, and six-and-twenty's gane. The lave o' my years are no' that lang that I'm ready to gae to bed at nine and lie like an auld maid chitterin' and listenin' to the win' – do ye hear't, Gibbie? Do ye hear't, Jock? It's got the deil's own spite at puir Mossgiel, and we're in a bit box, buried under snaw, three nameless bodies, and twa wi' the disease o' dull contentment. As for me, I'm choking, and I'm aff to Mauchline!"

He threw a plaid about him, scrugged down his bonnet on his brow, and made for the door.

"Poosie Nancy's, I suppose?" said Gilbert. "It's no' the best o' company ye'll get there."

"At least," said Burns, "they're no' ganting for their bed, or cloutin' brechams for their ain necks, and they'll no' be buried before their time!" and slammed the door behind him.

"Faith! he's in droll key, Rab, the nicht," said Blane, the ploughboy.

"It's pride," said Gilbert helplessly; "fair upsettin' vanity! Wealth's the warld's curse! He's awa' wi' his half-year's pay in his pouches – three pun ten!"

Mossgiel lay high on the breast of the brae and Burns for a moment stood at the door of it to look on Kyle below him blanched to a cold reclusive beauty by the snow. The sky was held by racing clouds, and the moon, at the full, fell giddily from space through the hurrying vapours, chased as in terror by her sweet young infant stars. Old trees overhung the dwelling, the tall haw-bushes made a hedge to shelter it; among them went the wind, that seemed to sweep the shire of Ayr of all its chilly elements and pile them, drift-white, in the wide quadrangle of the steading. Some sparks from the fire that Blane was banking for the night came up through the low chimney, and lived a moment red, aspiring little stars, that gave to the poet a fancy of his own and all men's sad futility; his heart played thud in his breast and he gasped with an emotion such as poets feel from things that may seem trivial to the world, but to the gifted have the import of a cataclysm. There was some spirit in the scene and hour – cold, pure, austere, remonstrant – that made him swither on the threshold, for he knew already that in the tavern he would find no higher uplift to his soul than came this moment from communion with the cleansed night. But still – but still, the sober face of the virtuous Gilbert ready for sleep, and the silence of the assiduous Blane, came back to him, and the sordid pot of tripe and thairm, and the dreary prospect of those waukrife hours in bed, with all his thoughts insurgent against slumber, and by comparison the barmy smells of Poosie Nancy's tavern, the feel of a pewter can, the gluck of poured ale, the loud dispute of hinds, and the admiration for his gifts of wit and clinking song-stuff, proffered an alternative that could not be resisted. He summoned the memory of other carousing nights to his weakening inclination for the ploy; stepped over the frozen duck-dub in the lane, and down between the mantled fields to the lighted village.

Upon these boozing peasants he made, in truth, but a rare intrusion. They felt half pleased and half disquieted, for though his presence was a kind of compliment, they had the start of him by several chappins, and they knew him for a man too apt to keep the crack on a level above the long-continued stretch of their ale-mused brains. His was the table-head, the fir-wood lug-chair; his the next round, his as many rounds as he cared to pay for; and the room of Poosie Nancy rang with a Bacchic symphony.

Before him, for a little, snow-white Kyle, the surging cloud and the moon intruded; in pauses of the trumpery conversation came across his mind that glance to the heart of things, that second's ecstasy he had found before the house on the brae, so that he almost rued the disposition that had brought him among this noisy crew. But one man had a story – not for parlours, witty, human, wicked, rich with the arterial blood of passion and grotesque of circumstance such as men heard then in Ayrshire even between the kirks; and another had a novel air with a ranting and resistless chorus, and the moon – the calm, clean, sovran moon – went down behind the clouds of vile tobacco, and over the remembered vision of the pure white fields was a mantle drawn, and the sound of the wind in the trees around Mossgiel was drowned in foolish chatter.

And yet he sought, as he sat among it, for those revelations of his loftier self, he drank with a deliberate purpose – not wholly for the warm sense of equality with these, his fellow-victims in the joke of Fate; for that rare elation, that confidence, that content, of which at times he had found the barley-fields possessed the magic key. Once he found it—in a thought that tore him from his company, a thought that only briefly kept a concrete form in the brain of him, then broke in a thousand iridescent pieces, each as precious as the whole, never to be brought together into something rational—a joyous, heady gambol through centuries of sun and storm; song, women, and the old lost fields of the youth he had never properly known, a sense of warmth, well-being, and perfection.

They had sung, among them, these dear hinds, his brothers, whom so well he understood, and pitied, one of his own songs, and this was his happy hour! A fiddle jigged in his brain, and Poosie Nancy's reeking chamber was transfigured.

Only for a space. The hour was late, right well had they scourged the gantrys for their ale; the morning hurried towards the fields of Ayr, and a woman stood beseeching for her husband, or his wages, at the door.

The man, the very boon companion who had started Burns's song, hung his head, and the shrill high voice of the vintner could be heard behind the wife's pathetic figure, proclaiming the respectability of her house, and her helplessness to quench the drouth of any man with the fate to belong to Tarbolton.

"Vive la bagatelle ! hae ye no' the money, Will?" said Robert Burns, and the man said, "No' a doit!"

"That's bad!" said Burns, with his fingers combing back the dank black locks from his burning brow; "ay man, that's damn bad! If I was a married man" – he laughed a little bitterly – "if I was a married man, I would likely still be Rabbie Burns; here, wife, it's a' that's left; it's aff-and-on thirty shillings; your man's a bonny singer and I'm for hame."

It was dawn when he came to the farm-house door, and Blane, the plough-boy, beat his arms across his breast ere he turned to mucking the byre. Kyle fell away below in billows of grey, and the cocks were crowing. The smoke of a green fire floated from the chimney-head, and the countenance of Gilbert, blameful and questioning, filled the door of the trance.

"Ye've had a nicht of it, Rab!" said he.

"I've had that, Gib!" said his brother peaceably.

"And what did it cost ye?" asked the keeper of the frugal conscience of Mossgiel.

"It cost me exactly three pun' ten, and cheap at the money," said the poet.

"On drink!" said Gilbert, horrified.

"Sae be't!" said Robert; "whether or no', I'll get the name o't."

Burns and
Clarinda

THE light of the afternoon came flooding through the windows; bathed Miss Nimmo's parlour in a golden radiance, and gave a mellow, pensive tone even to the poet's reverie. He sat with his face in the shadow, for he had not yet got rid of his rustic fears of these fine Edinburgh ladies, the very elegance of whose apartments contributed to his uneasiness. With any man living he could hold his own, but these unusual women – calm, confident, unabashed before the fervour of his eye; moving like swans, conversing like schoolmasters upon abstract things, witty, prone to mocking smiles – they were the very devil! He feared yet he adored them, since they had for him abundantly the one thing dear to poets and lovers – Mystery.

"A penny for your thoughts, Mr Burns," said the charming Mrs Maclehose, showing her drift-white teeth in a smile that seven or eight years ago had done terrific execution among the bucks at Edinburgh balls.

"A poet's thoughts are surely worth more than that, Nancy," said Miss Nimmo.

"It all depends," said Mrs Maclehose archly; "he might be thinking us very uninteresting after meeting such sublime examples of our sex as the Duchess of Gordon."

"A fine woman!" said Burns with some enthusiasm. "In her company I forget that she's a duchess and feel myself a duke."

"It'll likely be her awccent," drawled Mrs Maclehose, in a clever imitation of the Duchess's uncompromising Scots, and the charming mimic fell a little in his estimation; he liked his women, above all things, kind.

"It's an accent that some of the greatest in the land have respected from the lips of the Duchess of Gordon," said Burns, with a curious tension of the jaw and a flash of the eyes. "I'm a Scot myself."

"The very greatest!" said Mrs Maclehose, grasping the generous widths of her gown and dropping him a courtesy, half ironic.

She was a lovely woman, Mrs Maclehose, and Burns, with the sense of sex as keen as his poetic vision, regarded her in this playful mood with his old illusion that here might be the long-desired Ideal – the woman of whom one could never weary. She was short in stature, just the right height for the head to fit in the nook of his shoulder; with hands and feet small and delicate; fair complexion; flushed with health, with dancing eyes and a soft vivacious utterance. An air of elegance, refinement, grace, seemed to respire from her presence, and she could rise like a bird, and instantly, to the loftiest, most poetic fancy he cared to express. They did not breed that kind of woman in the shire of Ayr; at all events, he had never had the chance to meet them.

And she admired him – that with Burns, as with all sons of art, was the main thing! He knew she did, and what was better still, he knew it was not wholly for his poetry, of which she generally preferred what shrewder judgment would have told her were the poorest stanzas. She admired him for his fame and for his story, and most of all she plainly admired him as a Man. So far as women were concerned, the poet would sooner be loved for his legs than for his lyrics.

She admired him so much that he would have been quite at his ease with her, were it not for the presence of their hostess, Miss Nimmo, who too obviously realised the situation, and was amused at something.

"What are you smiling at?" asked Burns, when the visitor was gone in a rustle of silk, leaving a wake of lavender perfume, and for the poet a sense of deprivation. Miss Nimmo had come from the door with that sly and merry aspect which women assume when they mean to betray the weaknesses or follies of their sex.

"Nancy has asked me to take you to a dish of tea at her house on Thursday," she replied primly.

"I'll go!" said Burns emphatically.

"Of course, of course!" said the quiet little lady; "I kent you would go, and I said as much. Nancy's raptures were surely not to be altogether thrown away on you! You must be the proud man to excite such sudden adoration in our impressionable sex."

"A fine woman!" said Burns fervently.

"H'm! So's the Duchess of Gordon," was the reply of Miss Nimmo. "Do you know, I think, so far as women are concerned, you're gey and easy pleased," and she smiled up at him with her shrewd, pawky, plain little face, sadly disconcerting him, for he was not used to the subtleties of women who knew the game.

"What do you mean?" he asked suspiciously.

"I was thinking," said the old lady, "of a girl called Jean Armour," and she looked at him with penetrating and unflinching eyes.

"Easy pleased," said he, with a flush appearing on his pallid countenance. "Madam, if you knew Jean Armour –"

"My rural swain," said the lady, rapping him on the fingers with her fan, "you'll maybe can write braw poetry but there are things you do not understand. When I talked about your being easily pleased, I was not passing judgment on the girl I name, whom I have never had the honour to see, but thinking of what is due to her, and of the way that you forget, and of your readiness to interest yourself in any other bonny face that comes the way. It's wonderful to me, who ken women, how you clever men can be glamoured by a little flattery from any designing creature with a languishing eye – "

"You are hardly fair to your friend or loyal to your sex," said the poet, relieved and laughing.

"I like my friend in spite of her failings," said Miss Nimmo, taking snuff. "I have plenty of my own; and she was made by nature for the beguiling of silly men bodies like yourself. And I am so loyal to my sex that I cannot think but with compassion of the lassie Jean, in Ayr."

"I can think of her myself," said Burns, abruptly and uneasily. "I hope you haven't mentioned her to Mrs Maclehose?"

"It wouldna make muckle odds if I did – to Mrs Maclehose."

"Who is she? What is she?" eagerly pursued the poet.

"An honest married woman who has had a family of four," replied Miss Nimmo, with a faint malicious smile, and the face of the poet fell a little—a family of four was something of a staggerer!

"A widow?" he asked indifferently, remembering there had been no mention of a Mr Maclehose.

"In a fashion," said Miss Nimmo. "Grass. Her husband is in the Indies, and she hopes he'll bide there. Mean time it is plain she wants to keep herself in practice at the gallivanting. I'm touched at her raptures over your book; she must have raced through it unco fast, for she borrowed my copy at nine o'clock last night when she heard there was a chance she might see you here."

"She's clever enough to understand even my poor book at a gallop," said Burns, pulling down his embroidered waistcoat. "What time did you say was her tea?"

Miss Nimmo sighed. "Hech, sirs! and this is genius!" said she. "My Nancy's got a head like a fizzy drink, and a tongue like the clatter-bane o' a duck, and the Bard o' Caledon, forgettin' the 'true pathos and sublime' he writes so bonnily about, is just as easily made dizzy wi' her arts as if he were a writer's clerk. Ye read French?"

"Yes," said the bard, and she plucked a volume from the table and directed his attention to Voltaire's counsel to the Duchess of Richelieu:—

Ne vous aimez pas trop; c'est moi qui vous en prie,
C'est le plus sûr moyen de vous aimer toujours.
Il faut mieux être amis tout le temps de la vie
Que d'être amants pour quelques jours.

"Quite so!" said the poet; "it's long since I learned that philosophy for mysel', but what o'clock did ye say was the lady's tea?"

— ◆ —

She flew at Tam wi' furious ettle

An injured knee kept Burns to his lodgings for some days after this, and he missed the chance of drinking tea with Mrs Maclehose, on whose charms of person and mind he had the better opportunity for musing. One evening, after a succession of blythe and roystering visitors, in a state of pleasant exaltation he wrote the lady a letter, drafting it carefully first in the very best style of "The Elegant Letter Writer," on which he and Gilbert had one time modelled their correspondence.

I do love you, if possible, still better for having so fine a taste and turn in poesy (he wrote). I have again gone wrong in my usual unguarded way, but you may erase the word, and put esteem, respect, or any other tame Dutch expression you please in its place. I believe there is no holding converse or carrying on correspond-ence with an amiable woman — much less a GLORIOUSLY AMIABLE FINE WOMAN, without some mixture of that delicious passion whose most devoted slave I have more than once had the honour of being.

"That's the style for Mistress Blue-stocking!" he exclaimed complacently, as he read it over. "It wouldna be muckle use wi' Jean," and then, resuming his pen, he wrote these memorable words: —

Oh Clarinda! shall we not meet in a state, some yet unknown state of being where the lavish hand of plenty shall minister to the highest wish of benevolence, and where the chill north wind of prudence shall never blow over the flowery fields of enjoyment! If we do not, man is made in vain.

"By the Lord!" said he, "that's genius!" and taking another toddy went well pleased with himself to bed.

Next morning he read the still-unposted letter, and laughed. "Oh Robin! Robin! whatna Machiavelli!" he exclaimed. "And whatna dulcet key! ' Lavish hand of plenty,' by Gad! ' North wind of prudence'! 'Flowery fields of enjoy-ment'! Keep us! what transparent sophistry! It would make even Jean laugh, and Miss Nimmo, if she saw it, would be unco nippy. Oh, Rab! ye write a bonny letter!"

He took a penny from his pocket and tossed it.

"Heads," said he when it fell. "The letter goes, with north winds and flow-ery fields and a' the rest o't, I wouldna say but it's just the thing for Nancy Maclehose."

And so began the Clarinda correspondence.

The Making of Tam o' Shanter

It was a dirty day in mid-November. The roads of Nithsdale, after weeks of rain, were fetlock-deep with mire, and the gauger's pony, ten parishes and two hundred miles of roads like these to her credit for the week, was very weary. If she smelt her oats at Ellisland, she did not show it in the usual way by the quickened pace and the eager shudder of the withers; she had fallen from a canter to a trot, from a trot to a walk. The steam rose from her flanks, and the flakes of froth were washed from off her neck by the rain that fell continuously; her head hung low. On treeless slopes, seen dimly against vague horizons on that weeping afternoon, or rising over sky-lines thinly fringed with starved, wild, haggard pines; or again in the scanty winter woods, the pony and her rider might have seemed to an observer, had there been one, like the last survivors of some hopeless sally in the endless fight of man against unconquerable wilds. Sometimes she turned a sad complaining eye upon her master when she felt his heel.

He was weary himself – sick-tired to the very soul! It was not altogether the weariness of the flesh, for once that day, for a too brief hour, he had been mighty. Back beyond Dunscore, he had had the idea for a song at the sight of a girl who smiled upon him from a wayside steading, and suddenly he had felt the old fond rapture wakened and transported – not by the girl, for she was soon forgotten, but by that heady gush of song creation that tore through the brain at times, and made him feel eternal and gigantic. He had not found the words for the song beyond "Ae fond kiss and then we sever," but he had the sweet low wail of it somewhere in his head, and was content to give every pulse of his heart to the emotion that he knew from experience he should easily find the words for later on.

There and then he was not weary. There and then was he invincible, for to him without research had come the true divine elation, that exaltation of the soul he sometimes sought for in the bottom of a glass with old companions, only to find a coarser substitute. 'Twas then he knew he would not die, he could not die; that he was older than the hills, and would outlast them; that he had been admitted to the Secret; that he partook of God's delight in that ancient hour when He was happy, and in one evening filled the empty space with shining stars! The rare joy of his senses went to his very blood and bone, so that his limbs became like iron; he could have split the oak with Cyclop fingers, or hurled the boulders of the Nith over the Lowther Hills!

Now, in this miry afternoon, home-coming, an utter weariness possessed him, holding him in body less than in his spirit. Round him was a landscape that in summer and in sunshine always filled his mornings with a gladness to contemplate, but was now become most gloomy and portentous. The dripping little woods were full of creaking boughs and lawless shadows; the mist-wrapped braes, appearing so inimical and strange; the river so inhuman and so out of key with any mood of conflict, helpless, swirling to the Solway just because it must, without volition, as men swirl giddily through space and time — these fed the stark rebellion of his soul at the fate that mastered him. And he was come in sight of Ellisland, his farm. The place brought to his soul a pang as if the memory of an ancient sin had stung him. There it was, its steading bowered in trees, near the verge of the gravelly precipice that sank to the river's side, a poet's farm, God help him! — a visionary's choice, as if a man could harvest crops of shilfy-song or winnow a rent from evening sunshine!

Clarke, his ploughman, came ganting – suspicious sign! – from the barn to take in his horse. Burns put the reins in his hands and looked at him for a moment like a man that burst with tidings.

"Did ye ever hear tell o' Sisyphus, Will?" said he, and the ploughman stared at his master. "Man!" said he, "I think there used to be an auld packman wi' that by-name that gaed aboot Kirkmahoe when I was there —"

"Na, na, Will, that wasna my Sisyphus," said Burns. "Ye can aye let down a pack, and a pack's something wise like, but Sisyphus was a king in Corinth, and now he is in Hell, for doom to push a bowlder o' stane for ever up a hill where it winna bide. There's a lot mair joyous recreations I could think o' for a king, that ance was happy, and can mind, that still has all his faculties about him, and beholds, at his labour, the accursed truth. My God! My God!" The cry burst from him like a cry of Calvary, and over his fields he looked, his sodden cauldrife fields, so helplessly unprofitable, and at his cottage with its dripping thatch already rotting, and at his fowls that sheltered in the byre door. In his eyes flamed wild rebellion.

"The Globe at Dumfries again!" thought the ploughman, turning to lead in the mare.

Burns held him for a moment with his hand upon his sleeve. "Tell me this, Will," he demanded. "Are ye a contented man? Do ye sleep sound at nicht? Do ye mind auld things? Do ye ever think ye micht be better? Do ye see yoursel' the actual man ye are? Do ye meet wi' mony folk that understand ye? Have ye ever had but a glimpse o' a' the possible joys o' life, and seen them gaun by ye like Nith down there, wi' you stuck helpless on the bank?"

The questions poured forth from him in a spate; he stood with his plaid half-loosened, as eager in his manner as if his fate were in the answer.

"O, I'm no' complainin'," said the ploughman, whose mind had grasped but little of this fierce, bewildering catechism. "I'm no' complainin', I aye tak' my meat, and sleep like a peerie."

Burns looked in the broad red face with envy, his own pallid and drawn with inward pain.

"Ye're the lucky man!" said he, and then he started for from the cottage came an infant cry – piteous, pathetic, the protest of the soul that is torn from heaven for a space of years to suffer trial. A myriad fresh emotions shook the gauger as he listened, and last of all a gush of tenderness.

"In wi' the meare!" he said, and slapped her kindly on the shoulders.

Next day was Saturday. He stayed at home.

"What Sisyphus was this ye were haiverin' to Will Clarke about last nicht, Rab?" asked his wife. "He's been at Sisyphus a' this mornin', and jalousin' it's some new sang ye are makin'. I tell't him I never heard tell o' Sisyphus."

"And I wish to the Lord I had never heard tell o' him either, Jean," said Burns. "He's just a chiel in a book, that had a gey ill task to do, and did the best he could, but could never get it done, and kent he couldna."

"Are ye sure it was a man, Rab?" asked Jean Armour. "It's liker to have been his wife," and she started to rock the cradle, humming a country air.

Burns wrapped his plaid about him, for the day, though dry, was bitter cold. He went down before the house on a path that wound to a slip of holm, and walked by the river's bank, here overhung by trees. The melancholy of the night before was gone completely; the irrevocable past and Ellisland's cold, clammy acres – "the riddlings of the world" – were no longer like a black dog on his back, he was even in a mood to rejoice that after all he had made a poet's choice, if not a farmer's, when he picked on Ellisland. To his mind came a promise he had made to Grose the week before that he should write a poem about the Carrick witches.

Now, it was the way of Burns, when he would spur emotion to give truth and passion to his lines, to seek, not through his later years for the inspiration, but in those golden irrecoverable hours that seemed to have concluded with abruptness, when he turned his back upon the land of Ayr. Never in youth had he been, strictly speaking, happy; sordid needs and fierce rebellions; shame, ambition, inability, and pride, made in these early times, the texture of his being, and weighing now with then, his intellect would have convinced him his present state was vastly more enjoyable. But the heart, and not the head, was ever his adjudicator, and his heart invested hours by Doon with incommunicable grandeur, for no other reason than that there and then he had been innocent and young. All Kyle, in such reflections, was invested with a fond and pensive charm for whose surrender the most princely future could not make amends. He loved her very stones!

From Edinburgh parlours, Highland and Border wanderings, communion with his social and intellectual betters, he had nothing learned that was not his already when he walked behind the plough, and all the fervours, all the sweet illusions and enchantments which he gave a voice in song were harvested in Ayrshire.

Babbling river! – babbling Nith! – a fonder cry, a sweeter chuckle on the stones was in old Doon whereto this water of Dumfries recalled him. As on many a night, awake, an exile, and remembering, he followed her again through all her courses, from the great dark muirland reservoir, by deep ravines and Castle Downans fairy dells down into Alloway and the bay of Ayr. It was the sound of distant waters, and estranged, that sang through his imaginative ear this afternoon; the river Ayr herself swept through his retrospect—how blest was he to have been born upon her banks!

Old homes, each with a ghost of him yet tenanting its silence, still were standing where he left them, faithful to the streams he had deserted—Mount Oliphant, Lochlie, Mossgiel; and folk he knew who had been young with him, still breathed the native air.

Thus wrapped in the essential sentiment of youth and home from which the vivifying spirit of his music always came, he turned his inward gaze upon the earliest scene that had impressed his childhood eerilie—the ruin of Kirk Alloway, and in a flash beheld its possibilities for the thing he sought.

The old Kirkoswald legend, and the man of Shanter Farm! The story cried for more of fantasy and fun than it ever got in Mauchline taverns, and Douglas Graham was manifestly designed by Heaven to be its chief protagonist.

The sun, as it were in benediction on his essay, burst through the surf of clouds and poured illumination. Burns paced beside the river, muttering,

> "When chapman billies leave the street,
> And drouthy neebors, neebors meet,
> As market days are wearing late—

By God! I have it! It's the night and it's the weather, and the right lilt for a body startin' on an unco journey wi' nae convoy except a wheen o' witches. Mirk lanes and dreepin' thickets; glaur underfoot; an angry wife at hame; an awfu' lowe in the aisle of Alloway; the Brig o' Doon to cross, and Shanter seven miles awa!

> – market days are wearing late,
> And folks begin to tak' the gate.
> And we sit –

And we sit, and we sit – now what would we be sittin' daein'? Are ye there, Shanter? Ay, there ye are, auld Truepenny! What would ye be sittin' late for? Bowsing, of course !

> And we sit bowsing at the nappy,
> And getting fou and unco happy –

Rab, man! ye rascal, ye're fair started! If gaugin' was as easy!"

For hours he paced the sheltered holm attended by the shapes of men and fantasy created by his will. Below, the Nith went rushing to the Solway, in ignorance of the appointed end, but fearless. Green plovers wheeled and cried above his fields; when the sun was whelmed in clouds, the air was cold. But not for Burns, who, for his fever, loosed the grey plaid and gave his bosom to the wind. Tears came to him, and laughter; he fell on each fancy like a prize and clutched it till it took a shape in cadence and in rhyme, more often better blessed as are the noblest artists, thought and words were born together in his brain. A hundred times he went back on the lines completed, sometimes to enrich or chasten, but his aim was rather to maintain the whole in tone, as clouds are, and the forests, the colours of bays and ships, the sounds of storm, the choiring of the cherubim. And his imagination the more surely mastered him at every repetition, so that he shivered when

> The wind blew as 'twould blawn its last
> The rattling showers rose on the blast,
> The speedy gleams the darkness swallowed;
> Loud, deep and lang, the thunder bellowed.

He wept at his image of brevity of pleasure that

> – like the snaw, falls in the river,
> A moment white then lost for ever.

He saw before him

> – Doon pour all its floods,

and only for a moment woke to see that it was the Nith that thundered at the bend.

The sun was setting on the distant hills when the poet was done; a rookery went clanging home, and to his bosom flew content. To his mind came that great ease, that satisfaction which attends on inspiration met with open arms, not shunned for fear or indolence, nor for a second set aside until the work is done. 'Twas done! 'Twas good! He felt himself a king, and this was his golden hour. From the stuff of dreams, from the impalpable air, he had fashioned human characters, had made a little world of Scottish people with all their whims and humours, mystery and fears. Oh! he loved them, drunk or sober – he, their creator, he that wrought the miracle and brought them from the void. But more

Kings may be blest

he joyed that he had, in their making, maintained the deeper, greater, more abiding thing – the Symbol, the essential soul that makes all that is great in the art of man a microcosm, a miniature of the world – the world that cries with vast night-deep and interstellar tragedies, and stuns to think on, yet is no bigger than a nut! Ellisland's cold bankrupt acres? – Bah! How little did they matter! The glimpses of what had seemed a Paradise – Edinburgh and Clarinda, and the parlours lost? – a fig for them! The narrow ways, the hard, poor years in front, the shrinking store of money? – what matter if he died a beggar, he had lived this hour!

He went back by the river side, and in where the cradle rocked.

"Jean," he said, "I have made a poem."

The Democrat

The stores and arms of the smuggler's brig which the gauger Burns had boarded, sword in hand, on the previous day in the shallows of the Solway were being sold by auction in Dumfries. Cutlasses and brandy-kegs, muskets and marlin-spikes, were rapidly knocked down to peaceable burgesses who did not very much want them, but were rendered recklessly acquisitive by the humorous sallies of Jock Pender the auctioneer, who was using the smuggler skipper's pistol for a gavel, and kept a couple of men from Taylor's inn going briskly round the crowd with copious supplies of spirits, ale, and cake.

"And now, gentlemen," said the auctioneer, "we come at last to the bulky stuff; thae four cannon – genuine Carron; see the mark o' the foundry on them for yoursel's. For a nice bit decoration to a house wi' a plot o' grun in front, there's naething beats a pair o' cannon. They're a' the vogue the now in London. There they are — thirty two-pounders, scoops, sponges, rammers; mounted a' complete ! I've never had a finer lot o' stuff gae through my hands. They're worth twenty pounds a-piece if they're worth a penny, but I'll no' ask that for them; wha bids five?"

"Shillin's," cried Willie Armstrong the persistent humorist, and Pender turned upon him with derision.

"Man, Will," he said, "they're worth that just to look at; what you want's a pen-gun and a wheen peas to pap sparrows wi'. Come awa' wi' a wise-like offer."

"What the deil would I dae wi' them? "asked Armstrong, munching cake.

"Ye could stick them down before your door to frighten off your creditors," suggested the auctioneer, and the humorist withdrew discomfited to solace himself with draughts of eleemosynary ale.

Burns, who had never been to bed since he left the boarding party on the previous day, stood by the carronades with a foot upon a trunnion; a man with the heart to gush with tenderness for mouse or daisy ruined by his coulter, he yet had a love of arms, and kept upon his desk in the little closet in the Vennel the dirk of Balmerino. Arms were to him not cruel things for slaughtering, but the tools of valour, instruments of liberty, accoutrements of romance. Here they were, the carronades, grotesquely out of place in Pender's yard; squat, dumpy, silent, gaping with open throats for the breath of war. Nobody made an offer. He searched the faces round him for a sign that any one experienced his feelings at the sight of the degraded guns — not beautiful in themselves, but for him evocative of a sentiment as keen as he could get from morions and hauberks, he saw indifference; the good folk of Dumfries looked on this ordnance as so much useless junk.

"Three pounds for the lot," he rapped out, slapping his hand upon a muzzle.

"Thank ye, Mr Burns!" said the auctioneer. "Three pounds I'm offered for the lot, ony advance on three pounds? Going—going—gone!" And he brought the pistol down on the head of a harness cask.

"Oh, the devil!" said Burns, taken aback to have his impetuous bid so soon accepted. "What am I to dae wi' a battery in the Vennel?"

"Ye can gie them to the French," suggested the auctioneer and the face of the poet lightened

"Faith I can!" said he. "Vive la Revolution! I'll pack them aff the morn's morn," and he met the astonished and reproachful gaze of Bailie M'Kie with amused defiance.

The sale went on; the Bailie sidled up to Burns on the outskirts of the crowd and set about a delicate remonstrance. He was perhaps the only man within the burgh qualified to do it without offence, for he came from Ayr, was old enough to have been once the poet's father's friend, and the poet and he, at many Sunday skaillin' of the kirk, cracked fondly about Carrick, both convinced it was the bonniest region in the realm of Scotland.

"I havena seen ye for a fortnight gane, Robert," he began, scooping up a pinch of snuff with a tiny ivory ladle. "I hear that besides chasin' the runners, ye've been at Mossgiel wi' your brother Gilbert. How's the mother?"

"Gettin' gey frail," said Burns sadly. "I went up ane's errand just to see her. Ye wouldna ken her, Bailie – crined awa to a shadow! But still the pride o' life and the vanity o' the eye in her, thank God! As particular about the piping o' her mutches as she ever was. Man, I wish I had her spunk!"

"Ah, dear me!" said the Bailie pensively. "I mind o' Agnes on her marriage day; she was a dashing one! H'm! we're a' gettin' on in years. And what way's Gilbert? Is he keepin' fine?"

"Oh, Gilbert's strugglin' at it ! Ye ken yoursel what Mossgiel is? – a gey cauld clarty hole; there's nae fineness in't for ony tenant, no, nor in ony place in Ayrshire but for landlords."

"Yes, yes, I understand," said Bailie M'Kie. "Too true, Robert! Too true! But the market's risin'. And cauld and clarty, or no' cauld and clarty, I must say mysel' I aye liked Mossgiel."

"I'm like that myself about it," said the poet. "It broke my heart, God d—n it! but in these days I was free, and no' a slave o' Geordie's, rummaging auld women's cellars, Besides that, it was Ayrshire, and no' so many gutsy moneybags gaun on the Mauchline plainstanes as in this Dumfries. Did ye ever see a town wi' mair respect for Mammon or mair terror o' a man reputed to hae Whiggish sentiments? They're beginnin' to think that I have horns! Ye're magistrate o' a bonny toon, Bailie!"

Bailie M'Kie sniffed nervously. "About thae cannons, Robert," he remarked. "It's none o' my affair perhaps, but I kent your folk and I have a great respect for ye, so I hope ye're no' in earnest about sendin' thae things to the French. The Supervisor would be sure to hear o't."

Burns shrugged his shoulders. "Bailie," said he, "I have nae doubt that he will; there's a lot o' sneck-drawers about Dumfries to clype a' my political indiscretions to Corbet, but I canna help it, I would never be discreet, I abominate the very word; it has a Hanoverian smell. I ken fine a' the Corbies o' Dumfries are down on me because they understand I'm Jacobin, because I said George Washington was a better man than Pitt—and so he is, a thousand times! – and because I read the 'Gazetteer.' "

"Whisht! that's a' right!" whispered the Bailie, with a timid glance around to see that they were not overheard. "I whiles read the 'Gazetteer' mysel', and ye ken I'm as Whig as onything—in reason, Robert, in reason! but you're in the excise, drawin' your seventy pounds a year frae Geordie; ye should keep a calm sough and let independent men like Dr Maxwell or John Syme rant sedition. Think what ye like, man, but keep your mouth steeked; that's my advice to you, Robert!" and again he drenched himself with maccabaw, and turned away with apprehension that some gentry from the outskirts of the burgh were regarding them suspiciously.

Burns seized him by the shoulder. "That's the real sneck-drawin' policy, Bailie," he said, "and I'm no' fit for it. The guns are gaun to France the morn's mornin':–

> Heard ye o' the Tree o' France,
> 　　And wot ye what's the name o't ?
> Around it a' the patriots dance
> 　　Weel Europe kens the fame o't.
> It stands where ance the Bastille stood —
> 　　A prison built by kings, man,
> When Superstition's hellish brood
> 　　Kept France in leading-strings, man."

He clung to the arm of the affrighted magistrate while he hummed the unholy verse, then released him with a laugh and went home for dinner.

Sure enough, the cannons went next morning with a letter from the poet to the French Convention. The fact was bruited round the town before the twelve-hours' dram. The merchant folk were dubious that the prank was rather daring even for a harum-scarum poet, the gentry of the burgh were disgusted. He felt that week a polar rigour in the air; his closest friends were desperately busy, they were not to be found even of an evening at the Globe. "It's silly! Downricht silly!" said M'Kie one evening to him, having risked a first-rate civic reputation, even the prospect of the Provost's chain, by sneaking in the dusk to the poet's domicile. "I warned ye it was rank sedition and worse than that, it was throwin' awa guid money, for it's no to be expected that the French'll get the guns."

"That's what I told him!" said Jean Armour. "Three pounds thrown awa on silly nonsense! But Rab's sae heidstrong!"

"Ye've made an awfu' hash o't, Robert," said the Bailie, "and ye're bound to hae Collector Mitchell down upon ye. Everybody's talkin' o' your rebel principles and sayin' ye're a dangerous man, prepared to see even Britain go to wreck and ruin. I ken better, bein' a Mauchline man, and what I thought was that ye might come up to-morrow night to the Masons' meetin' and set things right sae far as possible wi' a stave o' the patriotic."

"What kind o' stave," the poet asked, smiling.

"Oh, ony kind o' trumpet stuff would serve for the occasion; ye could slap a couple o' stanzas up in half a jiffy; I would get them printed aff and circulated round."

"I daresay that!" said Burns. "Most kind of you! But I'm no' gaun to buy the gudewill o' Dumfries wi' patriotic stanzas made to order, Bailie, and your dainty bit plan would mak' me angry if it hadna got its comic side."

"Well, tak' my word for't, Robert," said the disappointed Bailie, "ye've made a bonny hash o' things, and may say 'fareweel' to the Friars Carse folk, Craigdarroch, Lawrie, and the ladies o' Woodley Park."

"Farewell and fair-good-e'en to them if that be so!" said Burns with a flashing eye; "I may doff my hat to them at times but no' my politics."

Bailie M'Kie was right too; only the tradesmen and artisans – Pyats as they onetime called them—could remain his friends. As in defiance, his political demeanour grew more boldly individual as time went on, and one night in the theatre when "God save the King" was played he sat and kept his hat on. "Turn him out!" "Shame, Burns!" cried the loyal citizens. Next day he walked the street alone, shunned by all but a few reckless revolutionaries, regarded with eyes askance.

He clearly realised the situation; now the air was worse than polar, having a sepulchral chill. Men who were proud to be seen walking with him some months ago transparently jinked now into quite inappropriate shops when they saw him coming. The most illuminating evidence of the state of things was to be seen in the ridiculous alarm of Brown, the saddler, who, coming hurriedly out of his shop with his brattie on to seek refreshment in a tavern across the way, turned and fled back like a startled hen at the very sight of Burns, whom he had so often joined in a post-meridian dram.

"Brown, too!" said the poet to himself with bitterness. "Well, poor soul! he has to think of his Dalswinton customers! And I should hae a bell about my neck — a leper's bell to let a' respectable, canny merchant-bodies ken that I'm on the street."

One man crossed and spoke to him—young Grierson, whom once he had befriended in a smuggling affair, a fellow with no character to lose. "Ye're takin' the air, Mr Burns?" he said politely, and the poet smiled a little ruefully.

"Ye see I'm welcome to as much of it as can be got on this side of the street," he said; "there's none of my fine friends over there inclined to share it." The ladies of Woodley Park and half a dozen lairds had that moment crossed the causeway to the other side with the obvious intention to avoid him.

"I thought ye were maybe makin' a sang," said Grierson sympathetically.

Burns shrugged his shoulders. "I got the drift o' ane to an auld air just now," he answered:–

"Policy parts good company.

The honest folk o' Dumfries are a' content to tak' the shady side o' the street because a Republican rogue tak's the liberty o' strollin' in the sun."

"It's thae d—n guns o' yours!" explained young Grierson impetuously. "What way do ye no' deny ye ever sent them?"

"It would be a lee if I did," said Burns. "I have lee'd wi' a glass, and lee'd – God help me! – wi' a lass, but I canna, drunk or sober, lee about my heart's convictions. Well, *vogue la galère*! – and that's French for ye, Jamie – come on and hae a dram!"

"Over to the Inn?" said Grierson agreeably.

"Nay, nay, young James! nae inns for us to-day! Too many o' my friends are there. Do ye ken Grizzel Baillie's ballad? –

His bonnet stood ance fu' fair on his brow,
His auld ane looked better than mony ane's new
But now he lets't wear ony way it will hing,
And casts himself dowie upon the corn bing.

O were we young, as we ance hae been,
We sud hae been galloping doun on yon green,
And linking it ower the lilly-white lea, –
And werena my heart light I wad dee!

"Only my heart's no' light, James; that's where the ditty fails me ... Where in a' the world are thae folk crowdin'?"

"Then ye havena heard the news!" cried Grierson astonished. "We're gaun to war wi' France; she threatens to invade us, and these are Volunteers. I joined mysel' an hour ago!"

— ◆ —

When Burns got home to his house in the Vennel, Jean, his wife, was baking scones.

"What's that on your hat?" said she; it had a bow of coloured ribbons.

"Great news!" he cried, elated. "The French are goin' to fight us, and I've joined the Volunteers. I wish to the Lord I had back my cannons!"

"Three pounds! And the children needin' boots! Ye're a braw poet, but there's whiles ye're awfu' stupid, Robert!" said Jean Armour. "And the French are goin' to fight us, are they? When are the puir deluded bodies goin' to start?"

"The sooner the better so far as I'm concerned," said Burns. "I'll be better wi' a gun than at the gaugin'. But the idiots up the toon imagine" – and he laughed – "that I'm no patriot!"

"If that's the case," said his wife as she cut the scones upon the griddle, "they canna hae read a great deal o' your poetry."

The Democrat

Finding Burns Online

Online versions of the works of Robert Burns are readily available, often in multiple instances. They come formatted as e-texts for e-book readers, or embedded in web pages, or as ordinary text files for use in wordprocessors. A huge amount of related information is also available, including glossaries of Scots words used in the poems, biographies of Burns, and descriptions of places, events and people associated with his life and works. Not all of this information is accurate; poems may be wrongly transcribed or incomplete, and biographical 'facts' may be spurious. It can be difficult to ascertain the quality of the material. Finding these resources on the web can also be a problem, due to the sheer volume of material that can be identified using a general search engine. Also, Robert Burns is not an uncommon name, and searches may retrieve material that has nothing to do with the man himself.

Librarians have a role to identify relevant, good quality resources for their customers, not just in the form of printed materials, but in any format, including online. The Scottish Library Association's website, SLAINTE, includes a catalogue of selected Burns material and a short biography taken from its publication, *Discovering Scottish Writers*. The catalogue records are linked to the resources themselves, which are just a mouse-click away. The records can be retrieved using the SLAINTE search engine, at URL http://www.slainte.org.uk/ slainte.html. Just enter the search term 'Burns, Robert 1759-1796' in the Names and Organisations option. Note that there are also many records for printed material, all held by the Scottish Poetry Library in Edinburgh, and many of which are available for loan or in-library consultation; see URL http:// www.spl.org.uk for further details.

The web can also provide access to online catalogues of printed Burns material held in libraries in Scotland and elsewhere. Until recently, it would have been necessary to search each online catalogue independently, using a variety of different interfaces, but the creation of Z39.50 'clumps' to create virtual, online union catalogues has made this much simpler. One such clump is the Co-operative Academic Information Retrieval Network for Scotland (CAIRNS), comprising all available catalogues that have the appropriate Z39.50 technology, including most of the university libraries and the National Library of Scotland. CAIRNS can be found at URL http://cairns.lib.strath.ac.uk/. A single search can be used for all or some of the CAIRNS catalogues simultaneously; it may be necessary to try the search terms 'Burns, Robert 1759-1796' and 'Burns, Robert' on the Author option in the Advanced searches facility of the service to ensure retrieval of all relevant records. Note that the SLAINTE catalogue is included in CAIRNS.

The CAIRNS service cannot incorporate catalogues that do not have the requisite technology, but many of these catalogues are available online for searching one-by-one, albeit with different search interfaces. It can be a daunting task, though, to have to search each one in the hope of finding significant quantities of Burns resources, and it might be better, in some circumstances, to identify which catalogues are likely to be useful before a search is carried out. A facility for doing this is available from the Scottish Collections Network (SCONE) service, at URL http://scone.strath.ac.uk/service/index.cfm. This allows a browse of names associated with collections; Burns is associated as the subject of a collection, or as the creator of items held in a collection. Bibliographic collections held by libraries, museums and archives are included. Specific Burns collections can be easily identified, and the service provides information such as the availability of catalogues (linked to the collection record where relevant), the address of the holding library, and opening hours. It may be possible to integrate SCONE and CAIRNS in the future.

Gordon Dunsire

Database Officer,
Scottish Library Association